Mindset Mathematics

Visualizing and Investigating Big Ideas

Jo Boaler

Jen Munson

Cathy Williams

T0366441

JOSSEY-BASS™
A Wiley Brand

Published by Jossey-Bass
A Wiley Brand
111 River St, Hoboken, NJ 07030
www.josseybass.com

Certain pages from this book are designed for use in a group setting and may be customized and reproduced for educational/training purposes. The reproducible pages are designated by the appearance of the following copyright notice at the foot of each page:

This notice may not be changed or deleted and it must appear on all reproductions as printed. This free permission is restricted to the paper reproduction of the materials for educational/training events. It does not allow for systematic or large-scale reproduction, distribution (more than 100 copies per page, per year), transmission, electronic reproduction, or inclusion in any publications offered for sale or used for commercial purposes—none of which may be done without prior written permission of the Publisher

Jossey-Bass books and products are available through most bookstores. To contact Jossey-Bass directly call our Customer Care Department within the U.S. at 800-956-7739, outside the U.S. at 317-572-3986, or fax 317-572-4002.

Wiley publishes in a variety of print and electronic formats and by print-on-demand. Some material included with standard print versions of this book may not be included in e-books or in print-on-demand. If this book refers to media such as a CD or DVD that is not included in the version you purchased, you may download this material at http://booksupport.wiley.com. For more information about Wiley products, visit www.wiley.com.

The Visualize, Play, and Investigate icons are used under license from Shutterstock.com and the following arists: Blan-k, Marish, and SuzanaM.

Library of Congress Cataloging-in-Publication Data

Names: Boaler, Jo, 1964- author. | Munson, Jen, 1977- author. | Williams, Cathy, 1962- author.
Title: Mindset mathematics : visualizing and investigating big ideas, grade 8 / Jo Boaler, Jen Munson, Cathy Williams.
Description: San Francisco : Jossey-Bass, 2020. | Series: Mindset mathematics | Includes index.
Identifiers: LCCN 2019045094 (print) | LCCN 2019045095 (ebook) | ISBN 9781119358749 (paperback) | ISBN 9781119358855 (adobe pdf) | ISBN 9781119358848 (epub)
Subjects: LCSH: Games in mathematics education. | Mathematics—Study and teaching (Middle school)—Activity programs. | Eighth grade (Education)
Classification: LCC QA20.G35 B638 2020 (print) | LCC QA20.G35 (ebook) | DDC 510.71/2—dc23
LC record available at https://lccn.loc.gov/2019045094
LC ebook record available at https://lccn.loc.gov/2019045095

Cover design by Wiley
Cover image: © Marish/Shutterstock-Eye; © Kritchanut/iStockphoto-Background
Printed in the United States of America

FIRST EDITION

PB Printing   SKY10034646_060222

Contents

To all those teachers pursuing a mathematical mindset journey with us.

Introduction

I still remember the moment when Youcubed, the Stanford center I direct, was conceived. I was at the Denver NCSM and NCTM conferences in 2013, and I had arranged to meet Cathy Williams, the director of mathematics for Vista Unified School District. Cathy and I had been working together for the past year improving mathematics teaching in her district. We had witnessed amazing changes taking place, and a filmmaker had documented some of the work. I had recently released my online teacher course, called How to Learn Math, and been overwhelmed by requests from tens of thousands of teachers to provide them with more of the same ideas. Cathy and I decided to create a website and use it to continue sharing the ideas we had used in her district and that I had shared in my online class. Soon after we started sharing ideas on the Youcubed website, we were invited to become a Stanford University center, and Cathy became the codirector of the center with me.

In the months that followed, with the help of one of my undergraduates, Montse Cordero, our first version of youcubed.org was launched. By January 2015, we had managed to raise some money and hire engineers, and we launched a revised version of the site that is close to the site you may know today. We were very excited that in the first month of that relaunch, we had five thousand visits to the site. At the time of writing this, we are now getting three million visits to the site each month. Teachers are excited to learn about the new research and to take the tools, videos, and activities that translate research ideas into practice and use them in their teaching.

Low-Floor, High-Ceiling Tasks

One of the most popular articles on our website is called "Fluency without Fear." I wrote this with Cathy when I heard from many teachers that they were being made to use timed tests in the elementary grades. At the same time, new brain science was emerging showing that when people feel stressed—as students do when facing a timed test—part of their brain, the working memory, is restricted. The working memory is exactly the area of the brain that comes into play when students need to calculate with math facts, and this is the exact area that is impeded when students are stressed. We have evidence now that suggests strongly that timed math tests in the early grades are responsible for the early onset of math anxiety for many students. I teach an undergraduate class at Stanford, and many of the undergraduates are math traumatized. When I ask them what happened to cause this, almost all of them will recall, with startling clarity, the time in elementary school when they were given timed tests. We are really pleased that "Fluency without Fear" has now been used across the United States to pull timed tests out of school districts. It has been downloaded many thousands of times and used in state and national hearings.

One of the reasons for the amazing success of the paper is that it does not just share the brain science on the damage of timed tests but also offers an alternative to timed tests: activities that teach math facts conceptually and through activities that students and teachers enjoy. One of the activities—a game called How Close to 100—became so popular that thousands of teachers tweeted photos of their students playing the game. There was so much attention on Twitter and other media that Stanford noticed and decided to write a news story on the damage of speed to mathematics learning. This was picked up by news outlets across the United States, including *US News & World Report,* which is part of the reason the white paper has now had so many downloads and so much impact. Teachers themselves caused this mini revolution by spreading news of the activities and research.

How Close to 100 is just one of many tasks we have on youcubed.org that are extremely popular with teachers and students. All our tasks have the feature of being "low floor and high ceiling," which I consider to be an extremely important quality for engaging all students in a class. If you are teaching only one student, then a mathematics task can be fairly narrow in terms of its content and difficulty. But whenever you have a group of students, there will be differences in their needs, and they will be challenged by different ideas. A low-floor, high-ceiling task is one in which everyone can engage, no matter what his or her prior understanding or knowledge, but also one that is open enough to extend to high levels, so that all students can be deeply challenged. In the last two years, we have launched an introductory week of mathematics lessons on our site that are open, visual, and low floor, high ceiling. These have been extremely popular with teachers; they have had approximately four million downloads and are used in 20% of schools across the United States.

In our extensive work with teachers around the United States, we are continually asked for more tasks that are like those on our website. Most textbook publishers seem to ignore or be unaware of research on mathematics learning, and most textbook questions are narrow and insufficiently engaging for students. It is imperative that the new knowledge of the ways our brains learn mathematics is incorporated into the lessons students are given in classrooms. It is for this reason that we chose to write a series of books that are organized around a principle of active student engagement, that reflect the latest brain science on learning, and that include activities that are low floor and high ceiling.

Youcubed Summer Camp

We recently brought 81 students onto the Stanford campus for a Youcubed summer math camp, to teach them in the ways that are encouraged in this book. We used open, creative, and visual math tasks. After only 18 lessons with us, the students improved their test score performance by an average of 50%, the equivalent of 1.6 years of school. More important, they changed their relationship with mathematics and started believing in their own potential. They did this, in part, because we talked to them about the brain science showing that

- There is no such thing as a math person—anyone can learn mathematics to high levels.
- Mistakes, struggle, and challenge are critical for brain growth.
- Speed is unimportant in mathematics.
- Mathematics is a visual and beautiful subject, and our brains want to think visually about mathematics.

All of these messages were key to the students' changed mathematics relationship, but just as critical were the tasks we worked on in class. The tasks and the messages about the brain were perfect complements to each other, as we told students they could learn anything, and we showed them a mathematics that was open, creative, and engaging. This approach helped them see that they could learn mathematics and actually do so. This book shares the kinds of tasks that we used in our summer camp, that make up our week of inspirational mathematics (WIM) lessons, and that we post on our site.

Before I outline and introduce the different sections of the book and the ways we are choosing to engage students, I will share some important ideas about how students learn mathematics.

Memorization versus Conceptual Engagement

Many students get the wrong idea about mathematics—exactly the wrong idea. Through years of mathematics classes, many students come to believe that their role in mathematics learning is to memorize methods and facts, and that mathematics success comes from memorization. I say this is exactly the wrong idea because there is actually very little to remember in mathematics. The subject is made up of a few big, linked ideas, and students who are successful in mathematics are those who see the subject as a set of ideas that they need to think deeply about. The Program for International Student Assessment (PISA) tests are international assessments of mathematics, reading, and science that are given every three years. In 2012, PISA not only assessed mathematics achievement but also collected data on students' approach to mathematics. I worked with the PISA team in Paris at the Organisation for Economic Co-operation and Development (OECD) to analyze students' mathematics approaches and their relationship to achievement. One clear result emerged from this analysis. Students approached mathematics in three distinct ways. One group approached mathematics by attempting to memorize the methods they had met; another group took a "relational" approach, relating new concepts to those they already knew; and a third group took a self-monitoring approach, thinking about what they knew and needed to know.

In every country, the memorizers were the lowest-achieving students, and countries with high numbers of memorizers were all lower achieving. In no country were memorizers in the highest-achieving group, and in some high-achieving countries such as Japan, students who combined self-monitoring and relational strategies outscored memorizing students by more than a year's worth of schooling. More detail on this finding is given in this *Scientific American* Mind article that I coauthored with a PISA analyst: https://www.scientificamerican.com/article/ why-math-education-in-the-u-s-doesn-t-add-up/.

Mathematics is a conceptual subject, and it is important for students to be thinking slowly, deeply, and conceptually about mathematical ideas, not racing through methods that they try to memorize. One reason that students need to think conceptually has to do with the ways the brain processes mathematics. When we learn new mathematical ideas, they take up a large space in our brain as the brain works out where they fit and what they connect with. But with time, as we move on with our understanding, the knowledge becomes compressed in the brain, taking up a very small space. For first graders, the idea of addition takes up a large space in their brains as they think about how it works and what it means, but for adults the idea of addition is compressed, and it takes up a small space. When adults are asked to add 2 and 3, for example, they can quickly and easily extract the compressed knowledge. William Thurston (1990), a mathematician who won the Field's Medal—the highest honor in mathematics—explains compression like this:

> Mathematics is amazingly compressible: you may struggle a long time, step by step, to work through the same process or idea from several approaches. But once you really understand it and have the mental perspective to see it as a whole, there is often a tremendous mental compression. You can file it away, recall it quickly and completely when you need it, and use it as just one step in some other mental process. The insight that goes with this compression is one of the real joys of mathematics.

You will probably agree with me that not many students think of mathematics as a "real joy," and part of the reason is that they are not compressing mathematical ideas in their brain. This is because the brain only compresses concepts, not methods. So if students are thinking that mathematics is a set of methods to memorize, they are on the wrong pathway, and it is critical that we change that. It is very important that students think deeply and conceptually about ideas. We provide the activities in this book that will allow students to think deeply and conceptually, and an essential role of the teacher is to give the students time to do so.

Mathematical Thinking, Reasoning, and Convincing

When we worked with our Youcubed camp students, we gave each of them journals to record their mathematical thinking. I am a big fan of journaling—for myself and my students. For mathematics students, it helps show them that mathematics is a subject for which we should record ideas and pictures. We can use journaling to encourage students to keep organized records, which is another important part of mathematics, and help them understand that mathematical thinking can be a long and slow process. Journals also give students free space—where they can be creative, share ideas, and feel ownership of their work. We did not write in the students' journals, as we wanted them to think of the journals as their space, not something that teachers wrote on. We gave students feedback on sticky notes that we stuck onto their work. The images in Figure I.1 show some of the mathematical records the camp students kept in their journals.

Another resource I always share with learners is the act of color-coding—that is, students using colors to highlight different ideas. For example, when working on an algebraic task, they may show the x in the same color in an expression, in a graph, and in a picture, as shown in Figure I.2. When adding numbers, color-coding may help show the addends (Figure I.3).

Color-coding highlights connections, which are a really critical part of mathematics.

Another important part of mathematics is the act of reasoning—explaining why methods are chosen and how steps are linked, and using logic to connect ideas.

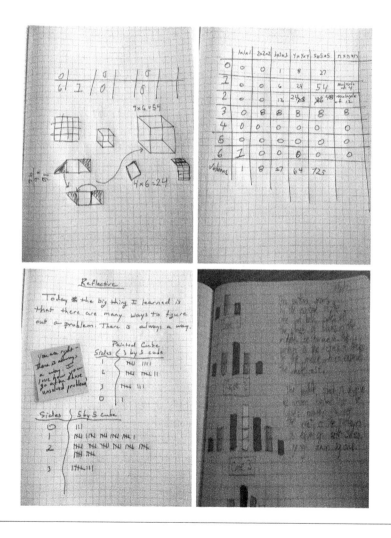

Figure I.1

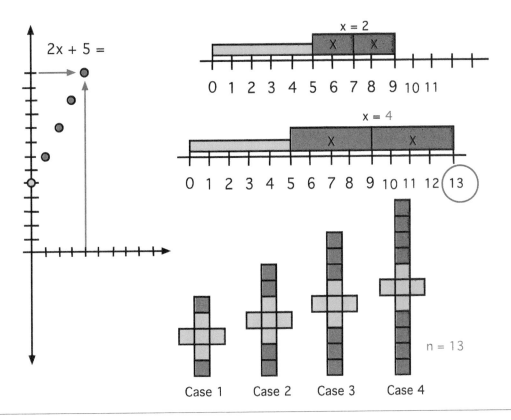

Figure I.2

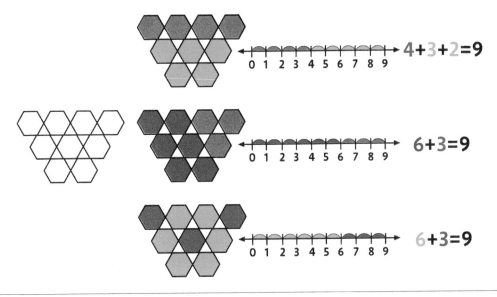

Figure I.3

Reasoning is at the heart of mathematics. Scientists prove ideas by finding more cases that fit a theory, or countercases that contradict a theory, but mathematicians prove their work by reasoning. If students are not reasoning, then they are not really doing mathematics. In the activities of these books, we suggest a framework that encourages students to be convincing when they reason. We tell them that there are three levels of being convincing. The first, or easiest, level is to convince yourself of something. A higher level is to convince a friend. And the highest level of all is to convince a skeptic. We also share with students that they should be skeptics with one another, asking one another why methods were chosen and how they work. We have found this framework to be very powerful with students; they enjoy being skeptics, pushing each other to deeper levels of reasoning, and it encourages students to reason clearly, which is important for their learning.

We start each book in our series with an activity that invites students to reason about mathematics and be convincing. I first met an activity like this when reading Mark Driscoll's teaching ideas in his book *Fostering Algebraic Thinking*. I thought it was a perfect activity for introducing the skeptics framework that I had learned from a wonderful teacher, Cathy Humphreys. She had learned about and adapted the framework from two of my inspirational teachers from England: mathematician John Mason and mathematics educator Leone Burton. As well as encouraging students to be convincing, in a number of activities we ask students to prove an idea. Some people think of proof as a formal set of steps that they learned in geometry class. But the act of proving is really about connecting ideas, and as students enter the learning journey of proving, it is worthwhile celebrating their steps toward formal proof. Mathematician Paul Lockhart (2012) rejects the idea that proving is about following a set of formal steps, instead proposing that proving is "abstract art, pure and simple. And art is always a struggle. There is no systematic way of creating beautiful and meaningful paintings or sculptures, and there is also no method for producing beautiful and meaningful mathematical arguments" (p. 8). Instead of suggesting that students follow formal steps, we invite them to think deeply about mathematical concepts and make connections. Students will be given many ways to be creative when they prove and justify, and for reasons I discuss later, we always encourage and celebrate visual as well as numerical and algebraic justifications. Ideally, students will create visual, numerical, and algebraic representations and connect their ideas through color-coding and through verbal explanations. Students are excited to experience mathematics in these ways, and they benefit from the opportunity to bring their individual ideas and creativity to the problem-solving and learning space. As students develop in their mathematical understanding, we can encourage them to extend and generalize their ideas through reasoning, justifying, and proving. This process deepens their understanding and helps them compress their learning.

Big Ideas

The books in the Mindset Mathematics Series are all organized around mathematical "big ideas." Mathematics is not a set of methods; it is a set of connected ideas that need to be understood. When students understand the big ideas in mathematics, the methods and rules fall into place. One of the reasons any set of curriculum standards is flawed is that standards take the beautiful subject of mathematics and its many connections, and divide it into small pieces that make the connections disappear. Instead of starting with the small pieces, we have started with the big ideas and important connections, and have listed the relevant Common Core curriculum standards within the activities. Our activities invite students to engage in the mathematical acts that are listed in the imperative Common Core practice standards, and they also teach many of the Common Core content standards, which emerge from the rich activities. Student activity pages are noted with a ⊕ and teacher activity pages are noted with a ⊕.

Although we have chapters for each big idea, as though they are separate from each other, they are all intrinsically linked. Figure I.4 shows some of the connections between the ideas, and you may be able to see others. It is very important to share with students that mathematics is a subject of connections and to highlight the connections as students work. You may want to print the color visual of the different connections for students to see as they work. To see the maps of big ideas for all of the grades K through 8, find our paper "What Is Mathematical Beauty?" at youcubed.org.

Structure of the Book

Visualize. Play. Investigate. These three words provide the structure for each book in the series. They also pave the way for open student thinking, for powerful brain connections, for engagement, and for deep understanding. How do they do that? And why is this book so different from other mathematics curriculum books?

Visualize

For the past few years, I have been working with a neuroscience group at Stanford, under the direction of Vinod Menon, which specializes in mathematics learning. We have been working together to think about the ways that findings from brain science can be used to help learners of mathematics. One of the exciting discoveries that has

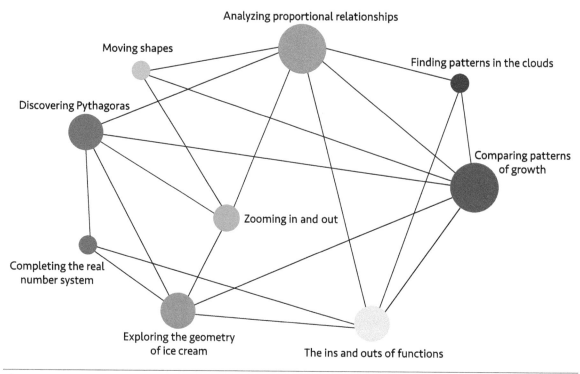

Analyzing proportional relationships

Moving shapes

Finding patterns in the clouds

Discovering Pythagoras

Comparing patterns of growth

Zooming in and out

Completing the real number system

Exploring the geometry of ice cream

The ins and outs of functions

Figure I.4

been emerging over the last few years is the importance of visualizing for the brain and our learning of mathematics. Brain scientists now know that when we work on mathematics, even when we perform a bare number calculation, five areas of the brain are involved, as shown in Figure I.5.

Two of the five brain pathways—the dorsal and ventral pathways—are visual. The dorsal visual pathway is the main brain region for representing quantity. This may seem surprising, as so many of us have sat through hundreds of hours of mathematics classes working with numbers, while barely ever engaging visually with mathematics. Now brain scientists know that our brains "see" fingers when we calculate, and knowing fingers well—what they call finger perception—is critical for the development of an understanding of number. If you would like to read more about the importance of finger work in mathematics, look at the visual mathematics section of youcubed.org. Number lines are really helpful, as they provide the brain with a visual representation of number order. In one study, a mere four 15-minute sessions of students playing with a number line completely eradicated the differences between students from low-income and middle-income backgrounds coming into school (Siegler & Ramani, 2008).

Our brain wants to think visually about mathematics, yet few curriculum materials engage students in visual thinking. Some mathematics books show pictures, but they rarely ever invite students to do their own visualizing and

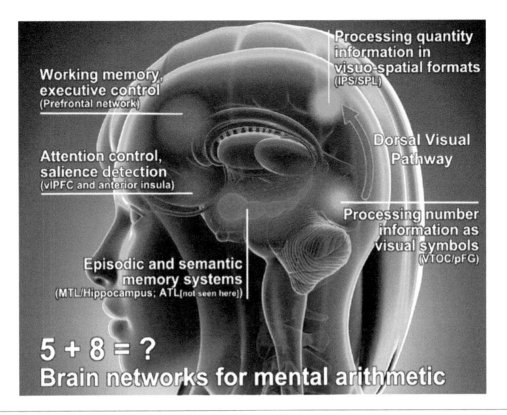

Figure I.5

drawing. The neuroscientists' research shows the importance not only of visual thinking but also of students' connecting different areas of their brains as they work on mathematics. The scientists now know that as children learn and develop, they increase the connections between different parts of the brain, and they particularly develop connections between symbolic and visual representations of numbers. Increased mathematics achievement comes about when students are developing those connections. For so long, our emphasis in mathematics education has been on symbolic representations of numbers, with students developing one area of the brain that is concerned with symbolic number representation. A more productive and engaging approach is to develop all areas of the brain that are involved in mathematical thinking, and visual connections are critical to this development.

In addition to the brain development that occurs when students think visually, we have found that visual activities are really engaging for students. Even students who think they are "not visual learners" (an incorrect idea) become fascinated and think deeply about mathematics that is shown visually—such as the visual representations of the calculation 18 × 5 shown in Figure I.6.

In our Youcubed teaching of summer school to sixth- and seventh-grade students and in our trialing of Youcubed's WIM materials, we have found

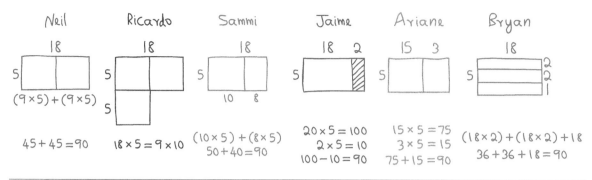

Figure I.6

that students are inspired by the creativity that is possible when mathematics is visual. When we were trialing the materials in a local middle school one day, a parent stopped me and asked what we had been doing. She said that her daughter had always said she hated and couldn't do math, but after working on our tasks, she came home saying she could see a future for herself in mathematics. We had been working on the number visuals that we use throughout these teaching materials, shown in Figure I.7.

The parent reported that when her daughter had seen the creativity possible in mathematics, everything had changed for her. I strongly believe that we can give these insights and inspirations to many more learners with the sort of creative, open mathematics tasks that fill this book.

We have also found that when we present visual activities to students, the status differences that often get in the way of good mathematics teaching disappear. I was visiting a first-grade classroom recently, and the teacher had set up four different stations around the room. In all of them, the students were working on arithmetic. In one, the teacher engaged students in a mini number talk; in another, a teaching assistant worked on an activity with coins; in the third, the students played a board game; and in the fourth, they worked on a number worksheet. In each of the first three stations, the students collaborated and worked really well, but as soon as students went to the worksheet station, conversations changed, and in every group I heard statements like "This is easy," "I've finished," "I can't do this," and "Haven't you finished yet?" These status comments are unfortunate and off-putting for many students. I now try to present mathematical tasks without numbers as often as possible, or I take out the calculation part of a task, as it is the numerical and calculational aspects that often cause students to feel less sure of themselves. This doesn't mean that students cannot have a wonderful and productive relationship with numbers, as we hope to promote in this book, but sometimes the key mathematical idea can be arrived at without any numbers at all.

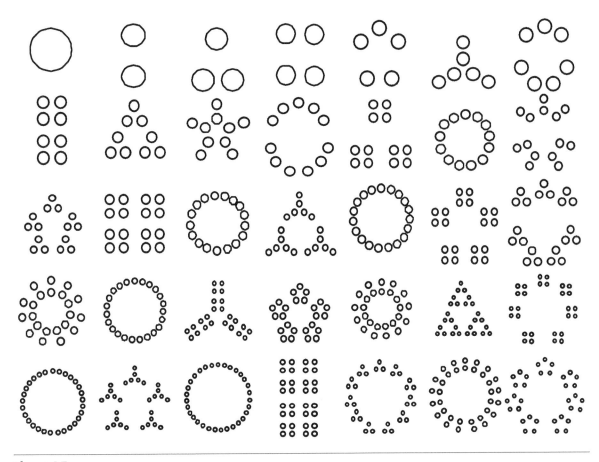

Figure I.7

Almost all the tasks in our book invite students to think visually about mathematics and to connect visual and numerical representations. This encourages important brain connections as well as deep student engagement.

Play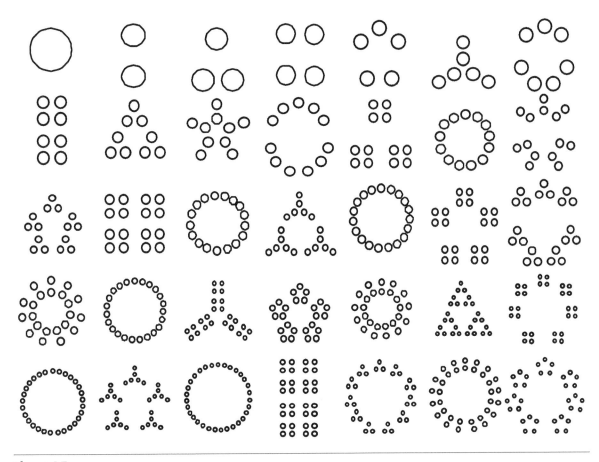

The key to reducing status differences in mathematics classrooms, in my view, comes from *opening* mathematics. When we teach students that we can see or approach any mathematical idea in different ways, they start to respect the different thinking of all students. Opening mathematics involves inviting students to see ideas differently, explore with ideas, and ask their own questions. Students can gain access to the same mathematical ideas and methods through creativity and exploration that they can by being taught methods that they practice. As well as reducing or removing status differences, open mathematics is more engaging for students. This is why we are inviting students, through these mathematics materials, to play with mathematics. Albert Einstein famously once said that "play is the highest form of research." This is because play is an opportunity for ideas to be used and developed in the service of something enjoyable. In the Play activities of our materials, students are invited to work with an important idea in a free space where they can enjoy the freedom of mathematical play. This does not mean that the activities do not teach essential mathematical content and practices—they do, as they invite students to work with the ideas. We have designed the Play activities to downplay competition and instead invite students to work with each other, building understanding together.

Investigate ❓

Our Investigate activities add something very important: they give students opportunities to take ideas to the sky. They also have a playful element, but the difference is that they pose questions that students can explore and take to very high levels. As I mentioned earlier, all of our tasks are designed to be as low floor and high ceiling as possible, as these provide the best conditions for engaging all students, whatever their prior knowledge. Any student can access them, and students can take the ideas to high levels. We should always be open to being surprised by what our learners can do, and always provide all students with opportunities to take work to high levels and to be challenged.

A crucial finding from neuroscience is the importance of students struggling and making mistakes—these are the times when brains grow the most. In one of my meetings with a leading neuroscientist, he stated it very clearly: if students are not struggling, they are not learning. We want to put students into situations where they feel that work is hard, but within their reach. Do not worry if students ask questions that you don't know the answer to; that is a good thing. One of the damaging ideas that teachers and students share in education is that teachers of mathematics know everything. This gives students the idea that mathematics people are those who know a lot and never make mistakes, which is an incorrect and harmful message. It is good to say to your students, "That is a great question that we can all think about" or "I have never thought about that idea; let's investigate it together." It is even good to make mistakes in front of students, as it shows them that mistakes are an important part of mathematical work. As they investigate, they should be going to places you have never thought about—taking ideas in new directions and exploring uncharted territory. Model for students what it means to be a curious mathematics learner, always open to learning new ideas and being challenged yourself.

* * *

We have designed activities to take at least a class period, but some of them could go longer, especially if students ask deep questions or start an investigation into a cool idea. If you can be flexible about students' time on activities, that is ideal, or you may wish to suggest that students continue activities at home. In our teaching of these activities, we have found that students are so excited by the ideas that they take them home to their families and continue working on them, which is wonderful. At all times, celebrate deep thinking over speed, as that is the nature of real mathematical thought. Ask students to come up with creative representations of their ideas; celebrate their drawing, modeling, and any form of creativity. Invite your students into a journey of mathematical curiosity and take that journey with them, walking by their side as they experience the wonder of open, mindset mathematics.

References

Lockhart, P. (2012). *Measurement*. Cambridge, MA: Harvard University Press.

Siegler, R. S., & Ramani, G. B. (2008). Playing linear numerical board games promotes low income children's numerical development. *Developmental Science*, *11*(5), 655–661. doi:10.1111/j.1467-7687.2008.00714.x

Thurston, W. (1990). Mathematical education. *Notices of the American Mathematical Society*, *37*(7), 844–850.

Note on Materials

In middle schools, we often find that there is little use of manipulatives and that few may be available in the building for teachers to choose from. But we believe, and extensive research supports, that all math learners benefit from mathematics that is visual, concrete, and modeled in multiple representations. Students need to physically create, draw, and construct mathematics to build deep understanding of what concepts represent and mean. Students need to interact with mathematics, manipulating representations to pose and investigate questions. Apps and digital games are another option, and we have found them to be valuable because they can be organized and manipulated with an unending supply. However, we want to emphasize that they should not be a replacement for the tactile experience of working with physical manipulatives. We support making different tools available for students to use as they see fit for the representation, and, following the activity, we encourage you to ask students to reflect on what the tools allowed them to see mathematically.

In our books for middle grades, you will find the same emphasis on visual mathematics and using manipulatives as in our elementary books, because these representations of mathematics are critical for all learners. If manipulatives are in short supply in your building, we encourage you to advocate for their purchase for the long-term benefit of your students. In the near term, you may be able to borrow the manipulatives we use in this book from your district's elementary schools.

Manipulatives and Materials Used in This Book

- **Snap cubes.** Snap or multilink cubes can be used for patterning, representing mathematical situations, and measurement. In eighth grade, we use them as tools for exploring and representing slope.

- **Square tiles.** Square tiles are flexible manipulatives that can be used to represent patterns visually that are too often only represented symbolically, making them a useful algebraic manipulative.

- **Cuisenaire rods.** Cuisenaire rods are mathematical manipulatives more common in elementary schools, where they are often used to represent part–whole relationships in operations and fractions. They can also be used like square tiles to represent some kinds of pile patterns or explore the Pythagorean theorem, which we offer as an option in eighth grade.

- **Fillable, relational geometric solids.** Geometric solids enable students to touch, rotate, and compare three-dimensional figures of different types. Some solids can be filled to explore volume. For eighth grade, we recommend a set of fillable relational solids that all have one dimension that is the same (height or diameter), so that students can fill and compare volumes.

- **Rulers.** We use rulers as linear measurement tools and as straightedges in the construction of graphs and geometric figures.

- **Meter sticks or yardsticks and balls.** As students investigate proportional relationships, we use meter sticks or yardsticks to create ramps that students can roll balls down to explore the relationships between how far the balls roll, the length of the ramp, and the height of the ramp.

- **Angle rulers or protractors.** Students need tools for measuring angles. Protractors are the most common tool, but are notoriously hard for students to use accurately. We prefer angle rulers, which have two arms that can be adjusted to fit an angle and are easier to read. They avoid the issue of needing to extend the sides of the angle being measured, which students encounter with protractors.

- **Compasses.** Compasses are tools both for drawing and for pivoting from a fixed point. In eighth grade, we use compasses to draw arcs and circles in geometric explorations. We use compasses to pivot when moving through an angle to explore rotations.

- **Colors.** Color-coding work is a powerful tool to support decomposition, patterning, and connecting representations. We often ask that students have access to colors; whether they are markers, colored pencils, or colored pens, we leave up to you.

- **Patty paper.** Patty paper is flexible and inexpensive, and it supports mistakes. Patty paper is a thin, transparent paper used in the food industry to separate food items. Its advantages in mathematics are that it is square paper that can be folded, cut, written on, and seen through for tracing or comparing. In eighth grade, we use patty paper to support explorations with transformations, enabling students to slide, flip, and turn figures and overlay them to look for congruence or similarity.

- **Calculators.** Calculators are used as a resource in the book to allow students to focus on the bigger mathematical ideas, rather than spending their time performing calculations. Calculators are a tool that students need to know how to use, and they should increase students' access to big mathematical ideas.

- **Office supplies, such as card stock, tape, glue sticks, and masking tape.** We use these across the book to construct charts, mark spaces, display thinking, or piece together work.

Activities for Building Norms

Encouraging Good Group Work

We always use this activity before students work on math together, as it helps improve group interactions. Teachers who have tried this activity have been pleased by students' thoughtful responses and found the students' thoughts and words helpful in creating a positive and supportive environment. The first thing to do is to ask students, in groups, to reflect on things they don't like people to say or do in a group when they are working on math together. Students come up with quite a few important ideas, such as not liking people to give away the answer, to rush through the work, or to ignore other people's ideas. When students have had enough time in groups brainstorming, collect the ideas. We usually do this by making a What We Don't Like list or poster and asking each group to contribute one idea, moving around the room until a few good ideas have been shared (usually about 10). Then we do the same for the What We Do Like list or poster. It can be good to present the final posters to the class as the agreed-on classroom norms that you and they can reflect back on over the year. If any student shares a negative comment, such as "I don't like waiting for slow people," do not put it on the poster; instead use it as a chance to discuss the issue. This rarely happens, and students are usually very thoughtful and respectful in the ideas they share.

Activity	Time	Description/Prompt	Materials
Launch	5 min	Explain to students that working in groups is an important part of what mathematicians do. Mathematicians discuss their ideas and work together to solve challenging problems. It's important to work together, and we need to discuss what helps us work well together.	
Explore	10 min	Assign a group facilitator to make sure that all students get to share their thoughts on points 1 and 2. Groups should record every group member's ideas and then decide which they will share during the whole-class discussion. In your groups . . . 1. Reflect on the things you do not like people to say or do when you are working on math together in a group. 2. Reflect on the things you do like people to say or do when you are working on math together in a group.	• Paper • Pencil or pen
Discuss	10 min	Ask each group to share their findings. Condense their responses and make a poster so that the student ideas are visible and you can refer to them during the class.	Two to four pieces of large poster paper to collect the students' ideas

Paper Folding: Learning to Reason, Convince, and Be a Skeptic

Connection to CCSS
8.G.3
8.G.4

One of the most important topics in mathematics is reasoning. Whereas scientists prove or disprove ideas by finding cases, mathematicians prove their ideas by reasoning—making logical connections between ideas. This activity gives students an opportunity to learn to reason well by having to convince others who are being skeptical.

Before beginning the activity, explain to students that their role is to be convincing. The easiest person to convince is yourself. A higher level of being convincing is to convince a friend, and the highest level of all is to convince a skeptic. In this activity, the students learn to reason to the extent that they can convince a skeptic. Students should work in pairs and take turns to be the one convincing and the one being a skeptic.

Give each student a square piece of paper. If you already have 8.5 × 11 paper, you can ask them to make the square first.

The first challenge is for one of the students to fold the paper to make a rhombus that is not a square and does not include any of the edges of the paper. They should convince their partner that it is a rhombus, using what they know about rhombuses to be convincing. The skeptic partner should ask lots of skeptical questions, such as "How do you know that the sides all have the same lengths?" and not accept that they are because it looks like they are.

The partners should then switch roles, and the other student folds the paper into a parallelogram that does not include any of the edges of the paper. Their partner should be skeptical and push for high levels of reasoning.

The partners should then switch again, and the challenge is to fold the paper to make an isosceles trapezoid, again not using the edges of the paper.

The fourth challenge is to make a trapezoid that is not isosceles. The trapezoid should be different than the one made in the third challenge. For each challenge, partners must reason and be skeptical.

When the task is complete, facilitate a whole-class discussion in which students discuss the following questions:

- Which was the most challenging task? Why?
- What was hard about reasoning and being convincing?
- What was hard about being a skeptic?

Activity	Time	Description/Prompt	Materials
Launch	5 min	Tell students that their role for the day is to be convincing and to be a skeptic. Ask students to fold a piece of paper into a square. Choose a student and model being a skeptic.	

Activity	Time	Description/Prompt	Materials
Explore	10 min	Show students the task and explain that in each round, they are to solve the folding problem. In pairs, students alternate folding and reasoning and being the skeptic. After students convince themselves they have solved each problem, they switch roles and fold the next challenge. Give students square paper or ask them to start by making a square. The convincing challenges are as follows: 1. Fold your paper into a rhombus that is not a square and that does not include any edges of the paper. 2. Fold your paper into a parallelogram that does not include any edges of the paper. 3. Fold your paper into an isosceles trapezoid that does not include any edges of the paper. 4. Fold your paper into a trapezoid that is not isosceles and does not include any edges of the paper.	• One piece of 8.5" × 11" paper per student • Paper Folding worksheet for each student
Discuss	10 min	Discuss the activity as a class. Make sure to discuss the roles of convincer and skeptic.	

Paper Folding: Learning to Reason, Convince, and Be a Skeptic

1. Fold your paper into a rhombus that is not a square and does not include any edges of the paper. Convince a skeptic that it is a rhombus.
   Reflection:

   Switch roles

2. Fold your paper into a parallelogram that does not include any edges of the paper. Convince a skeptic that it is a parallelogram.
   Reflection:

   Switch roles

3. Fold your paper into an isosceles trapezoid that does not include any edges of the paper. Convince a skeptic that it is an isosceles trapezoid.
   Reflection:

   Switch roles

4. Fold your paper into a trapezoid that is not isosceles and does not include any edges of the paper. Convince a skeptic that it is a trapezoid.
   Reflection:

BIG IDEA 1

Moving Shapes

In this book, we focus on a set of big ideas that extend across the eighth-grade curriculum, bringing in a greater focus on geometrical thinking. Geometry has been a neglected part of the eighth-grade curriculum for some time.

Ginsberg, Cooke, Leinwand, Noell, and Pollock (2005) investigated US students' geometrical experiences, looking at the international tests TIMSS and PISA, and found that US students spend 50% less time on geometry than students in other countries. Not surprisingly given this lack of attention, students' achievement in these areas was also significantly lower than students in other countries (Driscoll, DiMatteo, Nikula, & Egan, 2007).

Many teachers and students associate geometry with rules, remembering their high school years reproducing two-column proofs. This is the unfortunate outcome of a misguided approach to mathematics, when important ideas are lost as mathematical thinking is reduced to a set of rules. What is more critical to geometry is reasoning and adaptability. In this big idea, we introduce the ideas of congruence and similarity. Rather than just learning definitions for these, students look at cases and consider deeply the question, How do we know if two shapes are congruent or similar? Definitions play a part, but the most important act is reasoning; students should be encouraged to consider such questions as, What do we know now about this shape? What else do we need to know? Can I move or adapt my shape to give me more information? Can I convince someone else that my shapes are similar or congruent? What would I use to convince them? A great starting discussion for this sequence of lessons would be the question, What does it mean to be the same? Transformational geometry, congruence, and similarity are key ideas. We have chosen to focus our attention on triangles, the building blocks of geometric shapes and the coordinate plane, an important visual space for algebra.

27

In the Visualize activity, students are asked to consider the question, How do we know when two figures are the same? We ask students to study triangles where their vertices are provided. As students plot the points and connect the vertices with segments, they are asked to determine which triangles are congruent. We have created triangles that are congruent but may not appear so because they have been rotated and flipped. Others combine to make a triangle. Students can hone their detective skills by investigating each set. Students explore the key ideas visually.

In the Play activity, students are asked to transform shapes, rotating and reflecting them. We think that students will enjoy working out how one shape turns into another, developing patterns that explain the transformations. This is the work of computer animation, which has been important to the cartoon filmmaking industry for many years. Students will be given the opportunity to create their own puzzle transformations, which they can share with each other.

The Investigate activity provides students the experience of continuous transformations that are repeated over and over again. Students will be invited to design their own shape and think about what happens when they repeat the same transformation on the shape. In doing so, they will become pattern creators, which we hope they will find exciting. The work will help them understand what happens when transformations happen continuously, and the patterns that can result.

Jo Boaler

References

Driscoll, M. J., DiMatteo, R. W., Nikula, J., & Egan, M. (2007). *Fostering geometric thinking: A guide for teachers, grades 5–10.* Portsmouth, NH: Heinemann.

Ginsburg, A., Cooke, G., Leinwand, S., Noell, J., & Pollock, E. (2005). *Reassessing U.S. international mathematics performance: New findings from the 2003 TIMSS and PISA.* Washington, DC: American Institutes for Research and Department of Education.

What Does It Mean to Be the Same?

Snapshot

Using a set of coordinate pairs that describe triangles, students explore what makes two figures the "same" and develop a shared definition of *congruence*.

Connection to CCSS
8.G.1, 8.G.2

Agenda

Activity	Time	Description/Prompt	Materials
Launch	10 min	Show students the sets of coordinate pairs on the Point-by-Point Triangle sheet and ask them how they might figure out which of these triangles are the same. Discuss some initial ideas.	Point-by-Point Triangle sheet, to display
Explore	30 min	Partners map the triangle set onto a coordinate plane and explore which triangles they think are the "same." Partners develop a working definition of *same* for geometric figures and gather evidence to support which shapes are the same and which are not.	• Point-by-Point Triangle sheet, per partnership • Coordinate Plane sheet, per partnership • Make available: patty paper, rulers, and angle rulers or protractors
Discuss	15 min	Discuss which triangles students found to be the same and different, and the evidence they have to support these claims. Partners share the different working definitions they developed, and the class comes to agreement on a shared definition, which is then labeled as *congruence* on a class chart.	Chart paper and markers

To the Teacher

The core idea of this activity is congruence. We introduce students to geometric transformations by posing the question, How do we know when two figures are the same? The conventional definition says that two figures are congruent if you can obtain one from the other through a series of translations (slides), rotations (turns), or reflections (flips). That is, if you can slide, flip, or turn a shape and then lay it on top of another, such that the sides and angles align, then the two shapes are congruent. This excludes shapes that must be dilated to align; shapes that must be shrunk or expanded to align with one another are not congruent. We will return to dilations in Big Idea 2, which focuses on similarity.

This activity is designed to provoke discussion about what it means for two shapes to be the "same" and to provide an opportunity for the class to develop a definition of congruence. As part of gathering evidence for two triangles being the "same," we invite students to consider the corresponding points or vertices, or the related parts of two triangles being compared. The concept of corresponding sides and vertices of geometric figures reappears throughout geometry and is useful for decomposing the triangles in this activity to determine congruence. This may trigger the need to have names for the different parts of the triangles. We have given letter labels to the coordinate pairs that locate the vertices, and you can encourage students to use these to describe corresponding vertices. Students may not know how to describe the sides; if they are searching for ways to name these, you can tell them that it is a convention in mathematics to name sides by the two vertices that form the endpoints. For example, side AB ($\overline{AB}$) is between points A and B. It is not necessary for students to use formal language, but if they are struggling to describe their observations with precision, your providing language and teaching conventions can be useful.

Activity

Launch

Launch the activity by showing the Point-by-Point Triangle sheet. Tell students that the coordinate pairs in this table make triangles and that today their task is to figure out which of these triangles are the same. Ask, How could you do that? Give students a chance to turn and talk to a partner about a plan.

Invite students to share some initial ideas, but keep the conversation brief so that students still have plenty to think about. Point out that they will need to make a convincing argument for any shapes they believe are the same. If students raise questions about the meaning of *same,* you might tell them that deciding what it means to be the same is one of the goals for today's work and that they should think with their partner about what their definition of *same* will be.

Explore

Provide partners with the Point-by-Point Triangle sheet and the Coordinate Plane sheet. Make available patty paper, scissors, and angle rulers or protractors. Partners work together to map the triangles onto the plane and explore the following questions:

- Which shapes are the same?
- How could you prove it?
- If you find two shapes that are the same, which points (vertices) correspond?
- Which shapes are not the same? What is your evidence?
- What does it mean for two shapes to be the same?

As you talk with students, press them to develop a precise working definition of sameness that the class can discuss.

Discuss

Gather the class and discuss the following questions:

- Which shapes are the same?
- How can you convince us that two shapes are the same?
- Which shapes are not the same? What is your evidence?
- What does it mean for two shapes to be the same?

When you discuss these questions, press students to explain the kinds of evidence that are necessary to prove sameness or disprove it. When you discuss this final question, build a chart of criteria for sameness and name this idea as *congruence*. We expect that this discussion may generate some debate, and we encourage you to embrace disagreements while continuing to ask for reasoning.

- **Are partners accurately locating points on the coordinate plane?** Students may need to be reminded of the convention that coordinate pairs are given as (x, y) rather than (y, x). Transposing these is a common mistake. Interestingly, if students transpose all of the points consistently, they will still be able to explore congruence and make arguments about which shapes are the same and which are not. However, if students transpose some points, but not all, sometimes locating them as (x, y) and sometimes as (y, x), they will likely find no congruent figures.

- **Do partners have a clear and shared definition of** *same*? We expect that each group of students will develop their own definition of what is necessary for two figures to be considered the same and that these definitions will vary across the class. However, if students within a group are each using different criteria for sameness or their criteria are vague, they will not be prepared to make a coherent argument to justify which figures are the same. If you encounter students using vague or informal ways of determining sameness (such as, "They look the same"), ask, What is the rule for two figures being the same? Press them to develop a list of features, a test, or a definition that others could use. Students might also find it helpful to consider the evidence for difference. You might ask, How do you know that these two triangles are not the same? What are you noticing? Discussing contrasting cases can support students in naming the geometric features that could be relevant for defining congruence.

Reflect

How can you tell if two figures are congruent?

Point-by-Point Triangle

Triangle	Vertices
$\triangle ABC$	A(8, 8), B(8, 12), C(6, 8)
$\triangle DEF$	D(3, 6), E(−5, 10), F(−7, 6)
$\triangle GHI$	G(−4, 0), H(−4, 4), I(−1, 4)
$\triangle JKL$	J(5, 1), K(8, 1), L(8, −3)
$\triangle MNO$	M(−10, −11), N(−6, −3), O(−10, −3)
$\triangle PQR$	P(0, −4), Q(0, −7), R(4, −7)
$\triangle STU$	S(1, −12), T(9, −6), U(9, −12)

Coordinate Plane

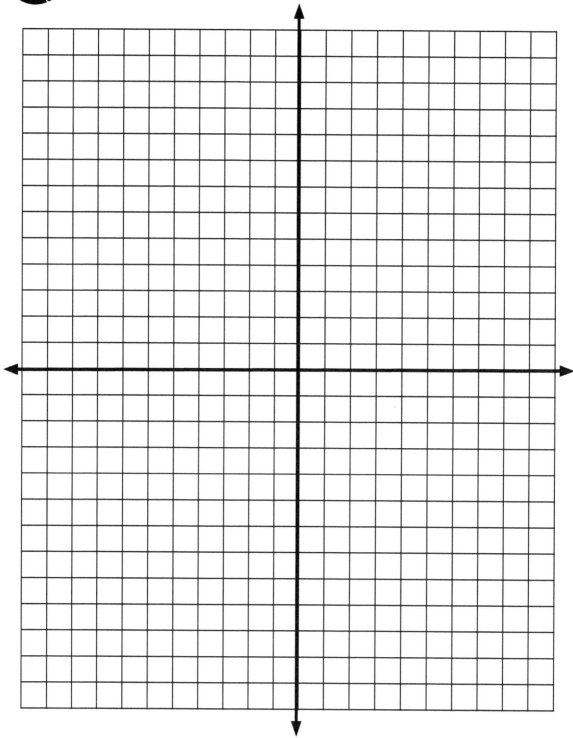

Pixel Puzzles

Snapshot

Students use pixilated designs on grids to analyze transformations and develop language for describing translations, rotations, and reflections. Students play with solving and designing transformation puzzles.

Connection to CCSS
8.G.1, 8.G.2, 8.G.3

Agenda

Activity	Time	Description/Prompt	Materials
Launch	5–10 min	Show students the figures on the Before and After sheet and invite them to describe how the figure changed. Discuss words for the type of transformation and the direction or magnitude of the transformation.	Before and After sheet, to display
Play	20 min	Partners work together to develop ways of describing the transformations shown on the Name the Change sheet.	• Name the Change sheet, per partnership • Make available: patty paper
Discuss	15–20 min	Discuss the ways that students described the transformations they analyzed. Develop a class chart that includes precise descriptions of the three types of transformations, connects these to the language students used, and includes words for describing direction or magnitude.	Chart paper and markers

Activity	Time	Description/Prompt	Materials
Play	30+ min	Partners play with a set of pixel puzzles on the Make the Change sheet, which challenge students to perform and undo transformations on patterns of their own design. When finished, students create their own puzzles on the DIY Transformations sheet.	• Make the Change sheet, per partnership • Patty paper, grid paper (see appendix), square tiles, and colors, per partnership • DIY Transformations sheet, as needed
Discuss	15 min	Discuss the strategies that students developed for understanding and performing different transformations. Discuss the challenges of reversing a transformation and the mistakes that emerged throughout the activity.	

To the Teacher

This activity is adapted from designs in Lou Kroner's *Slides, Flips, and Turns* (1994), which is sadly out of print. Although we often explore transformations with polygons, Kroner made use of patterns on grids, which provide a framework for comparing corresponding parts of the figures. The grids do not make it easy, though, and we think that students will find these pixilated designs challenging to transform. You may find that students are excited to make and test their own puzzles well beyond what we have offered here. With grid paper (see appendix), students can extend their play by making puzzles for themselves or each other.

The central idea in this activity is developing shared ways of describing transformations and understanding how these transformations look. In the first part of the lesson, we invite students to develop their own ways to describe changes, and we expect that you might hear a wide range of language for changes and directions, from "turn left" and "flip up" to "rotate counterclockwise 90 degrees." In the first discussion, make connections between the different ways that students are describing the same change. We encourage you to record these and their meanings in a chart. In the second part of the activity, students will likely run into questions about what it means to flip a shape vertically or horizontally, or what 90-degree, 180-degree, or 270-degree turns look like. Press students to reason through these questions, support one another in thinking about what it could mean, and use their experience in the first part of the activity as a reference. It is worth noting that with rotations, more than one way of describing the same transformation exists, as this may come up in discussions. For example, rotating a figure 90 degrees counterclockwise is equivalent to rotating the same figure 270 degrees clockwise.

Activity

Launch

Launch the activity by showing students the Before and After sheet on the document camera. Ask, What happened to the shape? How could we describe how it changed from before to after? Give students a chance to turn and talk to a partner. Take some examples of ways students describe the change. Be sure to draw attention to language that describes the nature of the change and language that describes direction or magnitude. There is no need to formalize the language students use at this point; you simply want to open the door to different ways that transformations might be described. Tell students that today they are going to play with describing and performing transformations using patterns on a grid.

Play

Provide partners with a Name the Change sheet and access to patty paper. Partners play with the strings of pixel puzzles, in which each row shows a series of transformations, to answer the following questions:

- What happened to the figure to go from one image to the next across the page?
- How can you describe it clearly? Can you find more than one way?

Students record in the boxes between figures their ways of naming the transformations so that they can discuss clear and precise ways of describing changes as a class.

Discuss

Discuss the following questions as a class:

- How did you describe the changes from shape to shape? (Embrace debate as you discuss each puzzle.)

- Are all slides (translations) the same? Why or why not? How can you describe the different types?
- Are all turns (rotations) the same? Why or why not? How can you describe the different types?
- Are all flips (reflections) the same? Why or why not? How can you describe the different types?
- When is there more than one way to describe the change?

Make a chart to formalize the names for translations (slides), rotations (turns), and reflections (flips), and show how these terms are connected to other language students have used to describe the same transformations. Include in your chart directional language that students come up with (left, right, up, down, horizontal, vertical, clockwise, counterclockwise, etc.) to moderate the types of transformations they saw.

Play

Provide partners with the Make the Change sheet, patty paper, grid paper (see appendix), square tiles, and colors. Ask students to first design a shape for the middle grid in each puzzle. Then partners determine what their figure would look like performing the two transformations moving forward (to the right) and how to reverse the transformations to find the original image (to the left).

When students finish, invite them to create their own patterns and rules to explore on the DIY Transformations sheet. Partners might each create a puzzle and swap, or work together to construct a puzzle for themselves or others to solve. Students might include some transformation directions in the labels and some pictures.

Discuss

Discuss as a class the following questions:

- What did you notice? What did you discover? (Discuss some of the individual parts to the puzzles.)
- What strategies did you use to slide, flip, or turn your designs? Which were most helpful, and why?
- What was hard about transforming these shapes? What did you struggle with the most? Why?
- What mistakes did you make? How did you notice your mistake? What did you have to do differently to address your mistake?

Be sure to discuss the challenges of reversing a transformation and how students thought through these parts of the puzzle. If students made puzzles for one another to solve, be sure to discuss how they had to think to design a puzzle, rather than just solve one.

Look-Fors

- **Are students moving their papers or using strategies for movement?** Surprisingly, we've found that many students want to perform transformations in their minds alone and devalue physical strategies for transformations or testing their ideas. If students struggle to visualize a rotation or a reflection, ask, What could you do to see how that transformation would look? What tools or strategies could you use? Encourage students to rotate their papers or to get up and look at their papers from a new angle. Students can make use of patty paper to perform reflections, or literally flip their papers over and hold them up to the light, so that they can see what a horizontal or vertical flip looks like. These are valid mathematical strategies for developing spatial reasoning, and students who engage in them will build skills for visualizing transformations.

- **Are students attending to corresponding parts?** As students record their transformations, they will need to pay attention to how each cell in the grid corresponds to a new cell in the adjacent grid. For instance, the top left cell may correspond to the top right cell after a flip or turn. You may notice errors in the figure, with cells moved inconsistently or with parts of a figure forgotten. As students map each figure onto a new grid, you might ask them, How do you know you have made the new figure accurately? What strategies are you using to check your thinking?

- **Are students reasoning about direction and magnitude?** With transformations, the description of the nature of the change isn't complete without some additional information about direction or magnitude. With a translation, students can simply describe it as up, down, left, or right, and in these puzzles, the direction is clear. But rotations and reflections are particularly challenging because they rely on language that isn't used every day, and students will have to reason about what it means to reflect vertically or horizontally and what it means to rotate a specified number of degrees and in which direction. Across this activity, press students to describe transformations as precisely as they can and to justify how they made sense out of a given transformation. Ask, How do you know to change the figure in this way? What does it mean to perform this transformation? Ask students to talk about all the parts of a transformation—not just flipping, but flipping how?

Reflect

Which transformation did you find trickiest to visualize? Why? What strategies did you use to help yourself?

Reference

Kroner, L. R. (1994). *Slides, flips, and turns*. Parsippany, NJ: Dale Seymour.

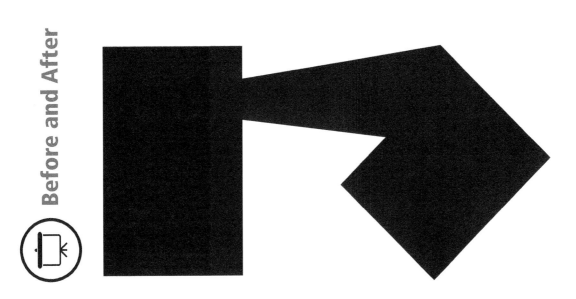

Before and After

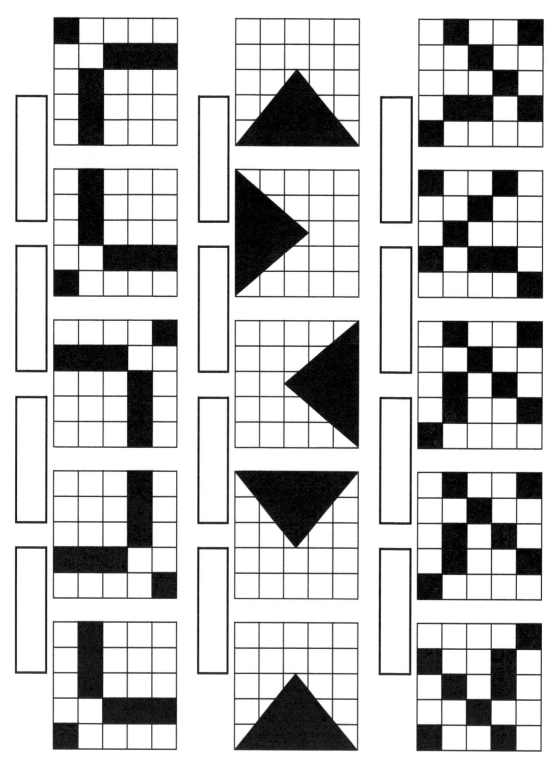

Make the Change

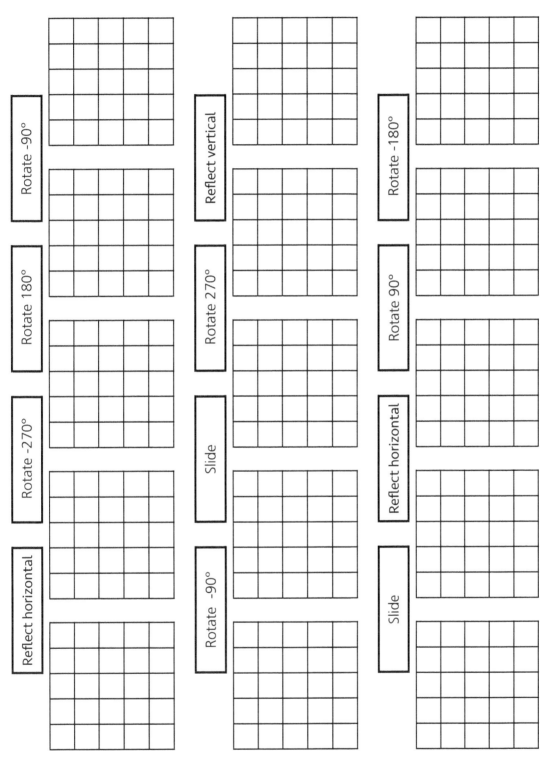

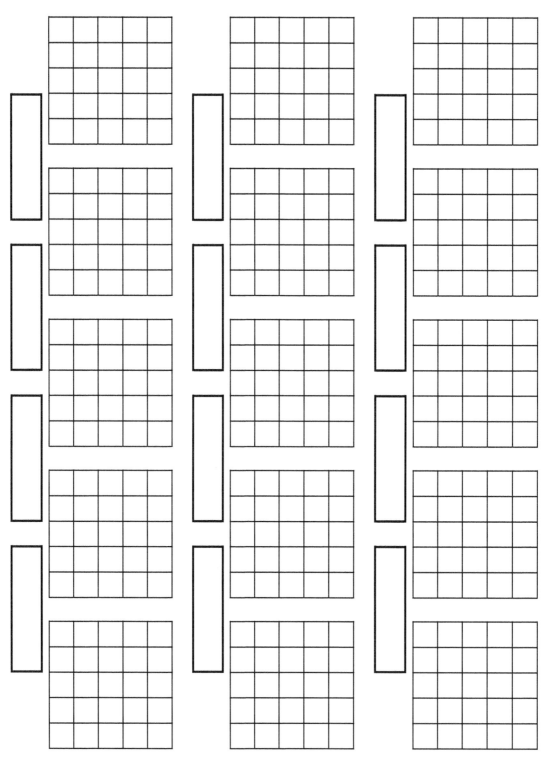

Slide It, Flip It, Turn It

Snapshot

Students investigate the patterns created by applying a transformation rule repeatedly to a geometric shape of their own design. Pooling their findings, the class looks for patterns in the kinds of rules that create different effects.

Connection to CCSS
8.G.1, 8.G.2, 8.G.3

Agenda

Activity	Time	Description/Prompt	Materials
Launch	5–10 min	Show students the Chain Pattern and discuss the different ways that students see and could extend it. Tell students that the rule for this pattern was a translation (or slide) of a certain number of units and this simple rule created repeating forms.	Chain Pattern sheet, to display
Explore	40+ min	Partners design a shape on dot paper and a rule for transforming it. Applying the rule repeatedly to the shape, students investigate the patterns created and why these might occur. Partners investigate different kinds of rules with different shapes to develop ideas about what transformations generate different kinds of patterns.	Make available: isometric and square dot paper (see appendix), rulers, compasses, patty paper, protractors or angle rulers, and colors
Discuss	15+ min	Post students' patterns in a display space and do a gallery walk. Discuss what kinds of rules generate different sorts of patterns, such as spirals or circles.	
Extend	Ongoing	Students hunt for transformation patterns in the world and bring in examples.	

To the Teacher

In this activity, we invite students to explore how a single transformation rule can create patterns when used repeatedly. We begin by looking at the Chain Pattern, which shows a series of overlapping triangles that was created with a rule that involved a translation to the right (or left, depending on how you look at it) a certain number of units. These now-overlapping triangles create new forms, such as rhombuses, and the pattern can continue forever to the left and right in a line.

An isosceles triangle, in blue, is duplicated and transformed
using a slide to the right.

More complex patterns are possible using rotations, reflections, and translations in combination. For instance, look at the pattern here. In this case, the rule for transforming the same shape was a slide to the right with a –30-degree rotation.

An isosceles triangle, in blue, duplicated with a slide and
a –30-degree rotation.

Both of these previous patterns could extend forever, but some patterns begin to overlap in such a way that nothing new is created. For example, the pattern here shows the same triangle being rotated 60 degrees around a fixed point. After five repetitions, the triangles overlap, and the pattern ceases to change.

An isosceles triangle, in blue, is duplicated five times.
Each duplication is rotated another 60 degrees.

Combining different transformations and exploring the results with different shapes is the focus of this investigation. Encourage students to try the same rule with different shapes, or different rules with the same shape, to see what results are attributable to the rule and which may be particular to a type of shape being transformed.

Some students may find this type of exploration particularly compelling given its connections to digital animation. As animators design movement, they must consider the algorithms, or rules, for repeated changes. When repeated transformations are seen in quick succession, they are perceived as smooth movement—for example, a car driving across the screen or a person turning their head. There are many intriguing online resources that explore the mathematics of animation, and we encourage you to support students in exploring these connections.

Activity

Launch

Launch the activity by showing the Chain Pattern on the document camera. Ask, How do you see this pattern? What would you draw to continue the pattern? Give students a chance to turn and talk to a partner. Discuss how students see the elements of the pattern. Invite them to come up to the document camera to point out how they see it and to show how they might draw it.

Point out that this pattern is made from transforming a shape. In this case, we've taken a triangle and repeatedly translated, or slid, it to the right some number of units. This rule created overlapping and repeating forms. Tell students that today they are going to experiment with transforming shapes to make patterns.

Explore

Make available materials for constructing and investigating transformation patterns, including isometric and square dot paper (see appendix), rulers, compasses, patty paper, protractors or angle rulers, and colors. Partners work together to draw a simple geometric figure on dot paper and create a rule for transforming it. The rule can be simple (one step) or compound (multiple steps). Be sure the rule is clear and includes both the type of transformation(s) and direction and magnitude language so that someone else could follow the rule. Students apply their rule repeatedly to the shape they have designed, drawing it on the same grid, as with the Chain Pattern example. Partners investigate the following questions:

- What happens? Why?
- What patterns are created when you follow your rule? Why?
- What interesting patterns can you make?

Encourage students to investigate another rule on the same or a different shape (or the same rule with a different shape) and continue to explore these questions. For every pattern created, ask students to label it with the rule used. Experiment with patterns by using color. How do different colors change what you see in the patterns you've made?

The same pattern with different colors

Discuss

Ask groups to post all of their patterns, labeled with the rule used, in a display space. Invite students to do a gallery walk and look for patterns across the patterns.

As a class, discuss the following questions:

- What kinds of rules make similar patterns?
- What kinds of rules make patterns that appear to end?
- What kinds of rules make patterns that could continue to grow forever?
- What rules created surprising patterns?
- How do different shapes change the appearance of the pattern?

You may want to work as a class to sort the patterns into groups based on common features, such as those that are circular, spiral, or linear. Sorting could support students in then determining what kinds of rules lead to these kinds of repeating patterns.

Extend

Students can extend their thinking about transformation patterns by investigating the question, Where in the world can you find patterns that were created with slides, flips, and turns? Encourage students to hunt in the school building, in architecture, in animation, in graphic design, art, tile work, cultural artifacts, and books. This could be an ongoing investigation, during which students are on the lookout for patterns and bring in examples or photos from their community, their reading, or the internet.

Look-Fors

- **Are students' rules specific?** The rules that students create need to be specific enough so that they (or another person) can follow them with precision. The rule description needs to include as many as four kinds of information: the type of transformation (slide, flip, or turn), the direction (up, down, left, right, horizontal, vertical, clockwise, or counterclockwise), the magnitude (the number of units or degrees), and the order (if students have more than one step, they need to specify which transformation is first, second, and so on). Ask students questions about their rules that support them in specifying each of these aspects of their rule, such as, What direction will you slide it? How far will you rotate it? Which comes first, the rotation or the reflection?

- **Are students' rules and shapes manageable?** Another issue that could emerge is that students may create a large shape or a rule that generates movement across a large distance, causing their pattern to skitter off the paper before they have a chance to see what happens. In these instances, ask, What happened? Why? Support students in pinpointing the issue. Then students need to decide how to handle it. They can either retain the shape and the rule, and tape multiple sheets of dot paper together to make a much larger surface, or revise the shape and/or the rule to make it more manageable. In either case, be sure to invite these students to share what they found with the class to add to everyone's learning about the results of transformations.

- **How are students dealing with challenges of rotation?** Rotating a figure is challenging, and the selection of the angle of rotation makes a difference in how complex that challenge is. On square dot paper, rotations of 90 degrees are more straightforward; on isometric dot paper, rotations of 60 degrees are supported by the grid. However, students may find that they want to explore smaller increments of rotation, such as 45 degrees or 30 degrees, and these will create more interesting patterns. As students are choosing an angle of rotation, ask, How will you use the dot paper to support you in rotating precisely? What other tools or strategies could you use? Students might, for example, use an angle ruler or protractor and patty paper to rotate through any angle.

Reflect

What did you discover that surprised you? What are you wondering now?

Chain Pattern

BIG IDEA 2

Zooming In and Out

This big idea captures a central concept in geometry, that of similarity. When students are thinking about similarity, as with other aspects of geometry, it is good for them to take on geometric "habits of mind." Mark Driscoll and colleagues (2007) offers a four-part framework that captures four productive mental habits, or habits of mind, when working with geometry.

Driscoll's Geometric Habits of Mind Framework
1. Reasoning with relationships
2. Generalizing geometric ideas
3. Investigating invariants
4. Balancing exploration and reflection

The first, reasoning with relationships, involves looking for relationships, such as similarity, the focus of this big idea, and thinking about how that relationship would help us understand the geometric figures being described. When reasoning, students should be encouraged to ask such questions as, What would I have to do to this object to make it like the other object? I like this question, as it highlights the active role that students can and should take, changing shapes and exploring the impact of their changes.

The second habit of mind, generalizing geometric ideas, is about seeking what there is about particular figures that would work in every case—what would be general. For example, if I double the lengths of the sides of a triangle, what else doubles? Do the angles double? Do the areas? Which relationships stay the same, and which change, in what ways?

The third habit of mind, investigating invariants, involves thinking about the aspects of figures that always stay the same—the aspects that are invariant.

53

When we transform figures, it is important to think about what happens to the shape. In Big Idea 1, students were repeatedly transforming the objects and thinking about what changed and what stayed the same.

The fourth habit of mind, balancing exploration and reflection, describes an approach whereby students try something out, but then stand back and take stock. As Driscoll points out, one characteristic of successful problem solvers is their meta-cognitive approach, balancing exploration with reflection, considering what they have discovered and learned.

These four habits of mind are very important in geometrical work, as they capture a reflexive relationship—acting on shapes and considering what is different and the same, reasoning about the shapes' properties, and stopping to reflect. These four habits of mind are useful in any mathematical work, but they are particularly important in geometry.

In our Visualize task, we have created an activity where students construct their own idea of what it means for figures to be similar. Typically students are given a rule for similarity and expected to remember it. We give them a different task: constructing the meaning of similarity through important visual thinking. Students are given similar triangles and asked, at first, to come up with their own definition for similarity and then to improve on it through class discussion. We bring the coordinate grid into the work, as this is a connection students rarely experience.

In the Play activity, students are presented with five images that look similar, and their job is to "find the fakes." They are then asked to make their own shapes to contribute to a "similarity carnival." This will enable other students to try to determine where the fakes are in different presentations of shapes. We think this will be an engaging way for students to encounter the idea of similarity and learn to reason and convince others of the similarity of figures.

In the Investigate activity, students look for similar figures that are connected and that overlap on a grid. This is a different, more complex presentation of similarity in which students are asked to unpack a complex shape. This should present important opportunities for struggle, as students typically find it hard to see the triangles and the similarity when the triangles are transformed.

Jo Boaler

Reference

Driscoll, M. J., DiMatteo, R. W., Nikula, J., & Egan, M. (2007). *Fostering geometric thinking: A guide for teachers, grades 5–10*. Portsmouth, NH: Heinemann.

What Is Similarity?

Snapshot

Using a set of similar triangles, students develop an evidence-based definition of similarity and apply it to constructing their own similar figures.

Connection to CCSS
8.G.4, 8.G.1

Agenda

Activity	Time	Description/Prompt	Materials
Launch	5 min	Show students the Similar Triangles sheet and tell them that these triangles are *similar*. Ask students what they think this might mean, and give them a chance to turn and talk.	Similar Triangles sheet, to display
Explore	30+ min	Using the figures on the Similar Triangles sheet, partners develop a working definition for *similar* figures and collect evidence from the examples to support this conjecture. Partners then apply their definition to create a set of similar figures.	• Similar Triangles sheet, per partnership • Make available: grid paper (see appendix), square and isometric dot paper (see appendix), rulers, and angle rulers or protractors
Discuss	20+ min	Partners record and post their definitions of *similar* for the class to read. Discuss how students arrived at these definitions, what they have in common, and where the class does not yet agree. Using evidence from the figures, come to agreement on a complete and specific definition for similarity, and create a class chart. Then invite students to share and discuss the similar figures they made and how they approached the task.	• Blank paper and markers, per partnership • Chart and markers

To the Teacher

The focus of this activity is crafting an evidence-based definition of similarity. Similar figures are congruent figures where one or more have been dilated—shrunken or stretched proportionally. Similar figures represent the intersection of geometry and proportional reasoning, and can ultimately be used as powerful tools for problem solving and pattern seeking. In this activity, support students in thinking about how the similar figures relate to the congruent figures they explored in Big Idea 1's Visualize activity.

Activity

Launch

Launch the activity by showing students the Similar Triangles sheet on the document camera. Tell students that these figures are *similar*, a word that has a mathematical meaning. Ask, What do you think *similar* might mean? Give students a chance to turn and talk with a partner to generate some thinking. Tell students that today, it is their task to use these examples to develop a definition for similarity.

Explore

Provide partners with the Similar Triangles sheet. Partners explore the shapes in any way they want in order to build a definition for similarity with evidence from the triangles. Partners develop answers to the following questions:

- What does it mean for two shapes to be similar?
- What evidence can you offer for your definition?

Once a group has a working definition of *similar* that all members agree on, partners use it to explore the question, Can you make your own set of similar figures? Make available grid paper and dot paper (see appendix), rulers, and angle rulers or protractors.

Discuss

Ask each group to record their definition of *similar* on a sheet of paper, large enough for others to read. Post these in a shared space where the class can read them.

As a class, discuss the following questions:

- How did your group come up with your definition?
- How do our definitions compare? What do we agree on? What do we not yet agree on? (You may want to mark on students' definitions the features that the class seems to agree on.)
- What evidence can we find in the similar triangles to help us come to agreement on a definition?

Be sure to chart a class definition of similarity, using the language agreed on through the discussion. After the class has a shared and specific definition of similarity that is supported by evidence, discuss the similar figures students made. Invite students to show their work on the document camera as you discuss the following questions:

- What similar figures did your group make? How did you do it?
- How did you know the shapes you made were similar?

Look-Fors

- **Are students identifying corresponding parts?** Students will need to use the spatial reasoning developed in Big Idea 1 to analyze how the figures have been rotated or reflected, so that they can identify corresponding parts. Comparing corresponding sides and angles is key to detecting what defines similarity. You might ask, How are these triangles related? How do the parts of this triangle correspond to the parts in that triangle? You may want to encourage students to develop ways of labeling these parts to show their relationships—for example with letters or color-coding.

- **Are students using measurement to compare the figures?** Similar figures have the same angle measures, but the side lengths are not the same; instead they are proportional in length. We have placed our triangles on a grid to support students in thinking about length and angles, though they will still need to use measurement tools for some angles and side lengths. Students may find an entry point simply by talking about how the figures *look* related. They are likely to name that the shapes are the same but different; support students in thinking more precisely by asking, What is the same? What is different? What parts or attributes? Encourage students to test their ideas about same and different by measuring to gather additional data.

- **Are students thinking proportionally?** In previous work on congruence, we had no need to quantify shapes; all that was necessary was to overlay the figures and see that they aligned. Similarity, however, relies on a quantifiable, proportional relationship between corresponding sides. It is mathematically sufficient, in the case of triangles, to say that corresponding angles are the same. But we want students to attend to the relationships that exist among the side lengths as well and connect these to ratio and proportion. Ask, How are the sides related? How could you compare them to see whether a relationship exists? Students might need to develop a way to organize their measurements so that they can compare corresponding parts. Ask, How can you organize your data to see whether there is a pattern to the side lengths?

Reflect

How can you tell when two shapes are similar?

Similar Triangles

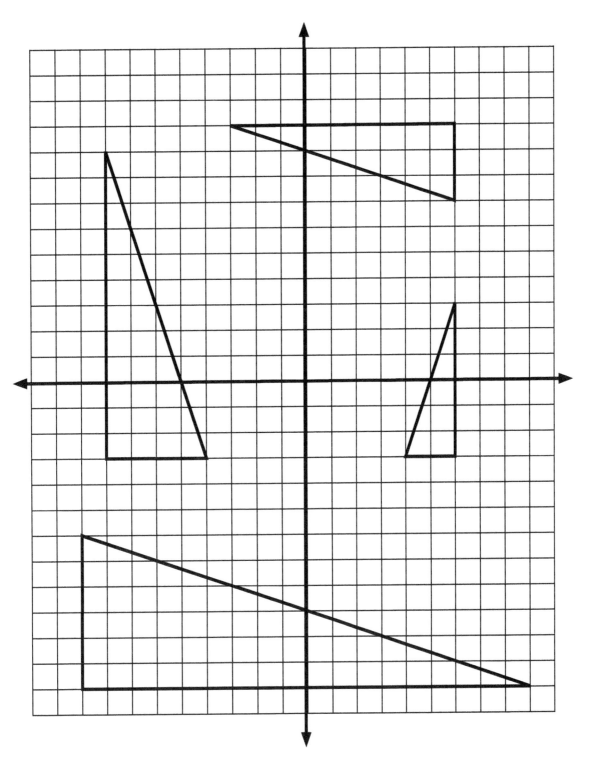

Find the Fakes

Snapshot

Students play with creating and detecting figures that are similar and not-quite-similar in a game of Find the Fakes.

Connection to CCSS
8.G.4

Agenda

Activity	Time	Description/Prompt	Materials
Launch	5–10 min	Show students the Find the Fakes sheet and tell them that some of these figures are similar to the original, and some are not. Ask students which they think might be fakes, or not similar to the original. Discuss students' intuitions.	Find the Fakes sheet, to display
Explore	40 min	Groups create a station for a game of Find the Fakes by creating an original figure and several others that are similar or nearly similar. Partners develop a justified answer key to ensure that their designs work as they intended.	Make available: grid paper (see appendix), isometric and square dot paper (see appendix), colors, rulers, protractors or angle rulers, scissors, tape, and chart paper
Play	20–30 min	Set up groups' stations and hold a similarity carnival, during which groups move between stations trying to detect which figures are not similar to the original. Groups keep records of their thinking and check their solutions against the stations' answer keys.	Groups' Find the Fakes stations positioned around the classroom

Activity	Time	Description/Prompt	Materials
Discuss	15 min	Discuss the strategies that students used to detect and construct fakes. Talk about the ways students used both intuition and mathematics to determine similarity (and not). Discuss the challenges students faced and the mistakes they made.	

To the Teacher

In our work thus far with transformations and similarity, we have focused activities on examining polygons. In this activity, we invite students to create their own figures as they play with similarity. These figures can be polygons or other geometric shapes, or they could be designs, animals, people, buildings, or anything else. We encourage you to let students be creative in their designs. Rather than holding students accountable for making a simple or efficient shape, hold students accountable only to the class definition of similarity created in the Visualize activity. We encourage you to have this chart posted for reference throughout this big idea. If students choose to create elaborate drawings, they will certainly find it more challenging to create similar figures. Some students may decide to revise their figures to make scaling them up or down more manageable. We consider these discoveries part of the exploration process.

Activity

Launch

Launch the activity by showing students the Find the Fakes sheet on the document camera. Tell students that some of the shapes are similar to the original figure (shaded), and some are not. Ask, Can you tell which figures are fake (or not similar to the original)? Give students a chance to turn and talk to a partner.

Ask the class, What does your intuition tell you? Discuss students' visual impressions about similarity. Students may describe something "being off" or "just not right" or "stretched" as their visual read on similarity. These visual impressions have value, but they can be deceiving. Tell students that today they are going to make and play with their own similar and nearly similar figures in a game of Find the Fakes.

Explore

Make available grid paper (see appendix), isometric and square dot paper (see appendix), colors, rulers, protractors or angle rulers, scissors, tape, and chart paper. Partners design a figure (shape, person, animal, or drawing) on a grid. Using this figure as their original, partners then create a set of similar and nearly similar figures for a game of Find the Fakes. Each group should make at least two similar figures and at least one near-similar fake, though they can make several more if they want to.

Each group makes a station with their original drawing and a set of labeled choices (A, B, C, etc.). Partners also need to construct a justified key that shows which figures are similar, which are not, and why. This key will help students check that their station works the way they intended. Stations can be a poster or just a collection of separate drawings. The original figure should be clearly labeled so that others know which figure to compare the others to.

Play

Set up groups' Find the Fakes stations around the classroom for students to play. Groups visit different stations and try to find the fakes, those figures that are not similar to the original. Tell students that when their group agrees on which figures are the fakes at the station, they can check the solution sheet made by the group who constructed the station. Groups should keep a record of their work at each station to support the class during the discussion.

It is not necessary for groups to rotate rigidly; rather, allow groups to move between stations as they finish and where there is space. Some stations and groups may take longer than others, and we encourage you to allow students to spend the time they need.

Discuss

As a class, discuss the following questions:

- What strategies did you use for finding the fakes? Which were most effective at detecting shapes that were not similar?
- What mistakes did you make? What tricked you?
- How did you use intuition? When you checked your intuitions mathematically, were they accurate?
- What strategies did you use for constructing your similar and near-similar figures?

Look-Fors

- **Are students constructing challenging stations?** Constructing two nonsimilar figures is not difficult; neither is detecting that two very different figures are not similar. For this task, the challenge lies in constructing figures that are similar and nearly similar, which leads to more puzzling work detecting which figures are and are not similar. Talk to groups about how they are constructing the nearly similar figures such that they are not obviously nonsimilar. You might ask, Can you tell just by looking which shapes are not similar? The flip side is that the figures cannot be so close to similar that it is virtually impossible, with the available measurement tools, to detect them. You might ask, How would another person be able to figure out that these are the fakes? Encourage students to revise their fakes so that they are detectable, but challenging.

- **Are students' fakes focused on proportion?** Students may become so focused on the design of their figures that they create a puzzle that is more akin to "Which one of these is not like the others?" by changing part of the design. For instance, students might remove a window from a house or change the color of the door. These cosmetic changes are not about similarity in the mathematical sense; they have nothing to do with proportionality. Ask questions about the near-similar figures such as, Why is this figure not similar to the original? Listen to the kinds of reasoning students provide. If students use evidence that is not about proportion, refer them back to the class definition of similarity and ask them which of the criteria the figure does not meet.

- **Are groups recording their evidence as they move between stations?** As students circulate through stations of Find the Fakes, they may be so focused on playing that they do not record their thinking. Students should keep a record of the stations they visit, any written work they do to test for similarity, the shapes they determine to be fakes, and the evidence they have for their decisions. As you circulate during the games, look at the ways students are recording their thinking, and encourage students to document their work so that they have something to refer back to during the discussion.

Reflect

What makes it hard to identify figures that are not quite similar?

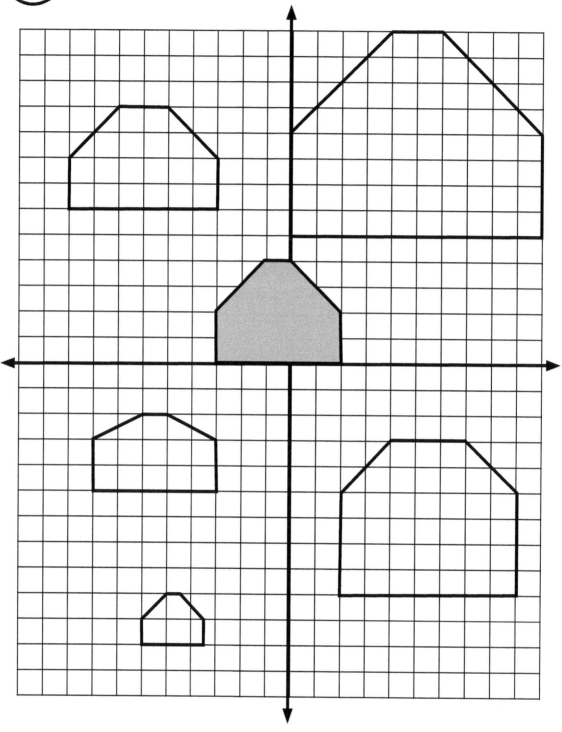

Growing on a Grid

Snapshot

Students investigate patterns in similar figures aligned on a coordinate plane.

Connection to CCSS
8.G.4, 8.EE.6

Agenda

Activity	Time	Description/Prompt	Materials
Launch	10 min	Show students the Growing Triangles sheet and tell them that these are similar triangles. Ask, How do you see the triangles growing? Discuss and record the patterns in the image.	• Growing Triangles sheet, to display • Optional: chart and markers
Explore	30–40 min	Partners construct their own sets of similar figures on a coordinate plane to investigate the question, Do all similar figures have the patterns we observed in the Growing Triangle image? Why or why not?	• Growing Triangles sheet, per partnership • Patty paper, grid paper (see appendix), ruler, protractor or angle ruler, scissors, tape, and colors, per partnership
Discuss	15+ min	Discuss the patterns students found and whether they were the same as, or different from, those in the Growing Triangle sheet and why this might be the case. Revise the class definition of similarity based on students' findings.	Class definition of similarity, from the Visualize activity

To the Teacher

In this activity, we invite students to explore similar figures as they overlap on a coordinate grid. By positioning the figures this way, we are planting the seed for connections between slope, similarity, and proportional reasoning. That is, similar figures have the same angle measures; when those angles are aligned, they create extending sides at the same angle, which can also be thought of as the same slope. In Big Idea 3, when slope is the focus, we will return to this idea and look for right triangles under a line, all of which will be similar because they share a common slope, or angle.

We are also introducing ways of thinking about geometry ideas that will resurface in high school math. Often students struggle when a geometric shape has a corresponding side or angle that is part of a similar or congruent shape. Having students experience these types of figures that are embedded within each other, overlapping, or combinations of other shapes is helpful for their later study of high school mathematics. Patty paper is a nice, inexpensive tool for tracing shapes from a diagram and manipulating them by rotating or flipping the shape to see that it is part of another figure. This work leads students to see the relative size of corresponding angles. In this activity, by anchoring the corresponding vertices at the origin, on the x-axis, and on a positive sloping line through the vertex, we are providing students an opportunity to make connections with overlapping similar figures. These overlapping figures directly relate to parallel line and angle postulates and theorems.

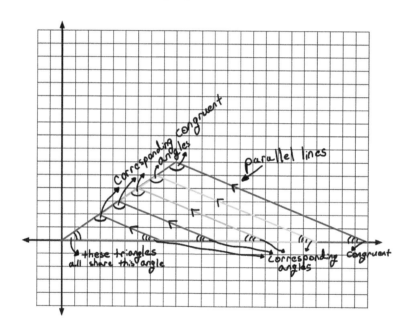

Activity

Launch

Launch the activity by showing students the Growing Triangles sheet. Tell students that this image shows a set of similar triangles. Ask, How do you see these triangles growing? Give students a chance to turn and talk to a partner. Collect students' ways of seeing the triangles grow. For instance, students may see the two aligned sides extending progressively, or they may see the growth as layers of trapezoids being added to the right.

Ask, What patterns do you see? As a class, discuss the patterns in this image and make a record of these patterns, either by annotating the image or making a chart.

Explore

Provide partners with the Growing Triangles sheet, patty paper, grid paper (see appendix), ruler, protractor or angle ruler, scissors, tape, and colors. Partners create at least one set of similar shapes on grid paper and position them on the coordinate plane.

- What's happening? What patterns do you notice?
- How would the patterns change if you aligned the shapes on a different angle? Why?
- Do all similar figures have the patterns we observed in the Growing Triangles image? Why or why not?

Discuss

As a class, discuss the following questions:

- What patterns did you find when you made similar shapes on the coordinate plane?
- Do all sets of similar figures produce the same patterns on the coordinate plane? Why or why not?
- How do different kinds of shapes (e.g., right triangles, parallelograms, irregular quadrilaterals) affect the patterns they produced?
- How might we revise our definition of similarity based on what we've discovered? (Return to the charted definition of similarity you began in the Visualize activity and revise or add on to the definition to reflect students' new findings.)

As you discuss these questions, invite groups to share the sets of similar figures they created as evidence to support or contradict conjectures about the patterns in similar figures.

Look-Fors

- **Are students' figures similar?** This investigation depends on students creating similar figures that can be overlaid on the coordinate plane. Students might use several different strategies of constructing similar figures, including those they developed in the Play activity. Ask students such questions as, How do you know your figures are similar to one another? What strategies did you use to create these figures? Students may create their similar figures independently on grid or patty paper, then transfer them to the coordinate plane. Any time that tracing or transferring is involved, error can be introduced. Ask, How do you know you are reproducing the figures accurately? Encourage students to use tools to promote precision, such as rulers and angle rulers, or to try to minimize transfer by simply taping their figures onto the grid instead of tracing them.

- **Are students attending to the coordinates to look for patterns?** Depending on the similar figures students created and the methods they used, they may have figures with vertices that fall at whole-number units on the coordinate plane. Indeed, you'll want to look for any groups that are constructing their similar figures directly on the coordinate plane to take advantage of the grid. If students have vertices that fall on whole-number coordinates, these can be a source of patterns. You might notice this aloud and ask students about it—for example, "I see that your vertices fall on the grid here. Do you think there are any patterns in the coordinates of similar figures?"

- **Are students seeing the sides of their figures as lines on the coordinate plane?** When students create similar figures individually in separate spaces, either on grid or patty paper, they will likely think of the sides of the figures merely as sides. However, when they begin to overlay them on the coordinate plane, we hope that students will see that two of the sides align in extending lines. These sides can then be thought of as lines that can continue forever, forming the sides of ever-growing similar figures. Once students have placed their figures on the grid and explored some of the patterns they produce, you might ask, How could you use these patterns to add new similar figures directly to your coordinate grid? Look for students extending the sides and developing ways of deciding how to place the remaining side(s) of their figure.

- **How are students making sense of the patterns in similar figures with more than three sides?** Encourage groups to explore sets of figures with more than three sides. Many groups will want to start with similar triangles, mirroring the Growing Triangles sheet. This is an appropriate entry point for determining whether the patterns we showed extend to other triangles. However, you'll want students also to explore quadrilaterals of different kinds and possibly shapes with more sides. When students create shapes with four or more sides, one vertex will be at the origin, two will be on the aligned sides, and any additional vertices will be sandwiched between. Ask, What patterns are there in where the fourth (or beyond) vertex is placed? Students may discover that invisible lines extending from the origin connect these vertices. These patterns are worth discussing with the whole class.

Reflect

How do you think similar figures might be useful? What kinds of problems could they help you solve?

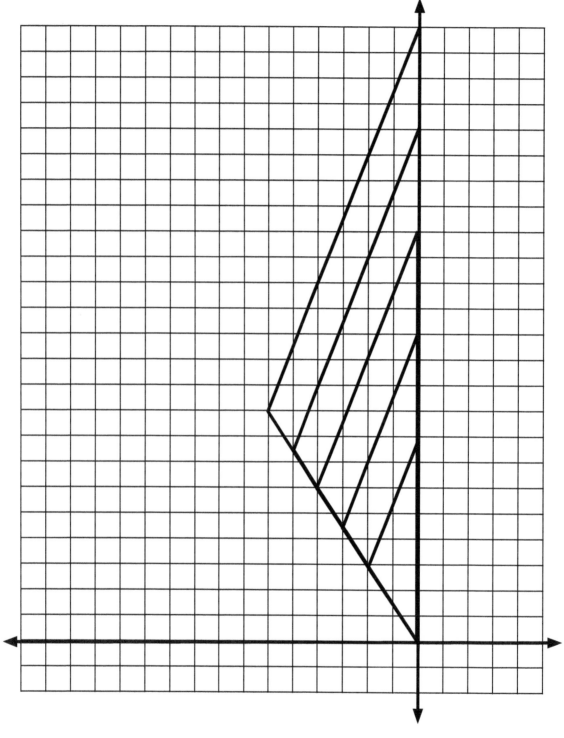

BIG IDEA 3

Analyzing Proportional Relationships

Proportions are a key idea in all of mathematics, and particularly in eighth grade. I recently read a lovely description of an important moment in mathematics history that centered on proportions, which was told by Cornell mathematician Steve Strogatz (2019) in his book *Infinite Powers*. The historical moment features one of the most important scientists in history, Galileo Galilei, an Italian astronomer, physicist, and engineer. As Strogatz describes, Galileo wanted to measure the speed at which objects fall, but in his time there were no video cameras or even accurate clocks. Galileo was not deterred by these challenges, and he set up an experiment. Instead of dropping a rock off a bridge, he allowed a ball to roll slowly down a ramp. To measure the time passing, he used a water clock. The "clock" allowed water to flow, and when he wanted it to stop, he closed a valve to stop the water flow. By weighing how much water had gathered, he could quantify the time passed.

Galileo made the ramp almost horizontal so that he could readily measure the speed of his falling object, measuring distance against time. This is when he found something incredible: the odd numbers 1, 3, 5, 7, and so on hide inside the falling of objects. Strogatz (2019) explains this, saying, "Let's suppose the ball rolls a certain distance in the first unit of time. Then in the next unit of time it will roll three times as far, and in the next unit of time it will roll five times as far . . . It's amazing; the odd numbers 1, 3, 5 and so on are somehow inherent in the way things roll downhill" (p. 67). Strogatz notes that he can "only imagine how pleased Galileo must have been when he discovered this rule" (p. 67).

There are many examples of mathematical patterns and sequences of numbers that emerge from explorations of real-life phenomena. I am always surprised and enchanted when I am exploring a pattern and Pascal's triangle of numbers falls out of it. Sequences of odd numbers inside the falling of objects is another example of mathematical beauty. As Strogatz (2019) reflects on the work of Galileo, "He coaxed a beautiful answer out of nature by asking a beautiful question" (p. 69). This moment in history marked the discovery of an important proportional relationship— speed. Proportions can be found throughout mathematics, and this big idea invites exploration into proportions inside triangles and rectangles.

In our Visualize activity, students investigate the relationships between three different triangles that come about when an altitude drawn to the hypotenuse decomposes a scalene right triangle into two smaller right triangles. Students discuss connections between proportionality and similarity using the three triangles they create. In a typical textbook question, students are given triangles and their measurements. We ask instead that students draw their own figures by following some explicit directions. They are then invited to discuss their figures, comparing and contrasting the triangles.

In our Play activity, students are given an image we call Seeing Triangles under the Line and asked to explore the right triangles that can be formed under the line, where the line is the hypotenuse. Students record the different triangles they see on the shared sheet. Students who investigate, like Galileo, will be rewarded with interesting patterns of numbers that emerge.

In our Investigate activity, we ask students to consider staircases! At first they look at some different staircases and consider their features, then they design their own. If doing so is possible at your school, students could experience staircases by walking them, thinking about such features as their height, length of tread, and slope. Students can build their staircases using snap cubes, blocks, square tiles, or similar, thinking about the central questions of slope, angles, and triangles. As students build and possibly walk staircases, the mathematical ideas of slope, measurement, and angles will develop in visual-spatial pathways in their brains. As they evaluate different staircases, they can discuss the big idea of proportional relationships where two quantities vary directly with each other and have a constant rate. You may even be able to find some staircases that are not built with a constant rate, which could prompt interesting discussions.

Jo Boaler

Reference

Strogatz, S. (2019). *Infinite powers: How calculus reveals the secrets of the universe* (Advance reading copy). Boston, MA: Houghton Mifflin Harcourt.

Dropping the Altitude

Snapshot

Students explore the relationship among three triangles created when an *altitude*, a line through one vertex and perpendicular to the opposite side, decomposes a scalene right triangle into two smaller triangles. Students use these triangles to discuss connections between proportionality and similarity.

Connection to CCSS
8.EE.6, 8.G.4

Agenda

Activity	Time	Description/Prompt	Materials
Launch	15 min	Show students the Triple Triangle Directions and ask them to create a sketch that follows these directions. Students compare drawings and, as a class, come to agreement on what a "right scalene triangle" is. Create a class chart with the terms *hypotenuse* and *altitude* diagrammed. Point out that dropping the altitude creates three triangles.	• Triple Triangle Directions sheet, to display • Whiteboard and marker, or note card, for each student
Explore	40+ min	Partners create multiple scalene right triangles that they cut along the altitude from the right angle to the hypotenuse. Students use these to explore the relationships between the three triangles created. Groups create a visual representation of their findings, using available tools, such as charts, slides, animations, or storyboards.	• Centimeter grid paper (see appendix), per partnership • Ruler, protractor or angle ruler, patty paper, and scissors, per partnership • Access to visual presentation tools, such as charts and markers or presentation software.

BIG IDEA 3: ANALYZING PROPORTIONAL RELATIONSHIPS

Activity	Time	Description/Prompt	Materials
Discuss	20+ min	Groups present their visual representations of their findings, and the class looks for shared patterns and contradictions. Discuss the relationships students found within the sets of three triangles they created and whether these patterns hold true across all scalene right triangles. Emphasize the language of proportion and the connection to similarity.	Students' visual presentations of findings

To the Teacher

In this activity, we continue to examine the tight connections between geometry and algebra we began looking at in Big Idea 2 by exploring proportional relationships within similar figures. In previous activities about similarity, students often knew at the outset that figures were similar or that they should determine similarity. In this activity, we simply ask students to look for patterns that connect three different triangles of their own construction. Using what they have learned about transformations and similarity, students discover that these shapes are similar, creating proportional side lengths.

We begin the activity differently than we have with others. Instead of showing students an image, we ask them to create one that meets two criteria. These criteria are given using some formal geometric language, so that the directions are precise. We've relied on language that students should have heard and used in previous grades, though they may not be fluent or remember the terms *scalene, perpendicular,* and *line segment.* These are more complex to interpret when given as a statement such as, "Draw a line segment from the right angle to the side opposite the right angle so that it is perpendicular to the opposite side." Rather than telling students what these terms mean or showing them how to follow these directions, we encourage you to devote a few minutes in the launch to allowing students to try to interpret and represent the directions. They will likely make mistakes, run into questions, and disagree with one another. Rather than entering the task with some students understanding, some misunderstanding, and some feeling stranded, the class as a group comes to shared understandings through their mathematical disagreements.

Activity

Launch

Launch the activity by showing students the Triple Triangle Directions on the document camera. Provide students with whiteboards or note cards for sketching. Give students a few minutes to try to interpret the directions and create a sketch.

Ask students to compare drawings with the person sitting next to them. Ask, Do you agree that you have followed these directions? Invite students to share drawings that do and, perhaps, do not meet the criteria listed. Discuss their reasoning and come to agreement on what "right scalene triangles" are and how to draw the *altitude,* or the line from the right angle to the *hypotenuse.*

Make a chart that shows these terms in a diagram of a scalene right triangle that students can use for reference. Point out to students that dropping this altitude creates three triangles: the original large triangle and two smaller triangles.

Explore

Provide partners with centimeter grid paper (see appendix), ruler, protractor or angle ruler, patty paper, and scissors. Partners explore the following question: When you drop the altitude from the right angle of a scalene right triangle, you create three triangles. What relationships exist among the three triangles you've created?

Partners create their own triangles to explore this question. Encourage students to start with large triangles to make comparing the smaller triangles easier. Partners test their ideas with multiple scalene triangles to see whether the patterns they find are consistently true.

Ask groups to make a visual display of their findings. Provide options for creating these displays, such as charts, slide shows, animations, storyboards, or other visual tools you might have available.

Discuss

Groups present their visual displays of the relationships they found. As the class watches these presentations, ask students to be looking for similar findings, or those that contradict. Be sure to discuss any contradictions and what those might mean.

As a class, discuss the following questions:

- What relationships did you find among the three triangles you created?
- Are these relationships true no matter what scalene triangle you start with? How do you know? How could you prove it?

In the discussion, emphasize the proportional relationships that students find, and use the language of proportions to name what students find. Draw connections between this language and similarity.

Look-Fors

- **Are students creating sets of triangles that meet the criteria?** As you observe students working, look and listen for struggles with the vocabulary of the directions for constructing sets of three triangles. There are multiple terms used in coordination that can be challenging to visualize. Our aim is that the discussion during the launch will support students in making sense of the criteria for constructing a scalene right triangle and dropping the altitude; however, you may still see students constructing triangles that do not meet these criteria. This is not intended to be a test of vocabulary; instead, we want to support students in making sense of these terms, how they are used together, and what they represent physically. You might ask students to talk you through how they constructed their figures or show you why they meet the criteria. Support students in pinpointing any mistakes and coming up with a plan to revise their diagrams.

- **Are students using multiple properties of the shapes to look for patterns?** In this activity, we ask students to look for as many relationships as they can find. Students may quickly identify one relationship, such as that corresponding angles are equal, or students may decide the figures are similar, and stop. Press students to find multiple, specific relationships, even if they all stem from similarity. They might examine angles and side lengths, or even area. They might go beyond finding that the figures are proportional and name the scale factors from one figure to the next. If groups declare they are done, you can always ask, What other relationships could there be?

- **Are students using the language of proportionality?** Coming out of Big Idea 2, students are primed to look for and recognize similarity. We hope this language comes up and that students see these relationships. However, listen for students using words like "proportional" to refer to the side lengths, and ask questions about proportionality, such as, How do you know they are proportional? Will the side lengths always be proportional when you construct a scalene right triangle and drop the altitude? Ask students who are already using this language to be sure to include it in the presentation of their findings.

Reflect

How are proportions and similarity connected? Draw a diagram to support your explanation.

1. Sketch a right scalene triangle.

2. Draw a line segment from the right angle to the side opposite the right angle so that it is perpendicular to the opposite side.

Seeing Triangles under the Line

Snapshot

Students explore the right triangles that can be formed under a line on the coordinate plane, where the line is the hypotenuse, planting the seed for understanding slope.

Connection to CCSS
8.EE.6

Agenda

Activity	Time	Description/Prompt	Materials
Launch	10 min	Show students the Seeing Triangles under the Line sheet and ask them what right triangles can be formed under the line, where the line is the hypotenuse. Students record on the document camera the different triangles they see.	• Seeing Triangles under the Line sheet, to display • Colors
Play	30+ min	On a coordinate plane, partners draw a line that passes through the origin and explore the triangles that can be formed under the line. Students look for patterns and try to use these to predict points on the line beyond the limits of their paper. Students play with these patterns by exploring new lines to see what relationships are true regardless of the line.	• Grid paper (see appendix), per partnership • Rulers and colors, per partnership • Make available: patty paper, overhead transparencies, or page protectors, and the appropriate markers

Activity	Time	Description/Prompt	Materials
Discuss	15 min	Partners share the many ways they saw right triangles under the lines they drew and the relationships they found among them. Discuss whether right triangles formed under a line will always be similar, and why.	

To the Teacher

In this activity, we begin to connect similar triangles, proportion, and slope. Students play with the right triangles they can draw under a line on a coordinate plane, where the line is the hypotenuse.

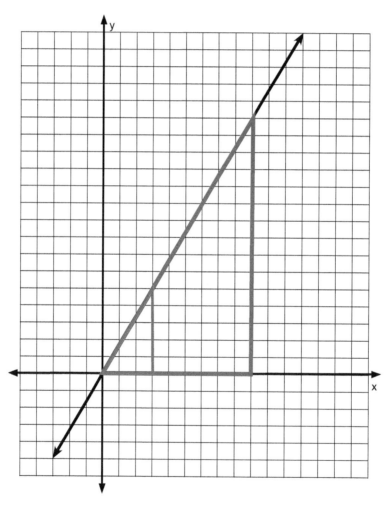

Under the $y = \dfrac{5}{3}x$ line, similar right triangles can be formed.

An infinite number of right triangles can be drawn under any given line, and they will all be similar because they have the same slope. This slope fixes the two acute angles of the right triangle, so that in all right triangles drawn, corresponding angles will be congruent. This pattern previews an idea that students will return to in high school geometry: the angle-angle similarity postulate, which states that if two corresponding angles of two triangles are congruent, the triangles are similar. Students do not need to know these formal principles, but they can engage with the ideas of similarity, angle, and slope using what they have already learned.

Building on the techniques students used to explore similarity, we recommend that you have tools available for students to record, move, and overlay the triangles they find. Any material that students can use to record and can see through will work, such as patty paper, old overhead transparencies, sheet protectors, or wax paper. These enable students to make a triangle and slide it up and down the line to see that it works in infinite positions along the line.

Activity

Launch

Launch the activity by showing students the Seeing Triangles under the Line sheet on the document camera. Ask, What right triangles can you see under this line, where the line is the hypotenuse? Give students a chance to turn and talk to a partner about what they see. Invite students to come up to the document camera and draw, in different colors, the right triangles they see. Tell students that today they are going to explore the right triangles that can be formed under a line on the coordinate plane.

Play

Provide students with grid paper (see appendix), ruler, and colors. Make available tools for overlaying triangles, such as patty paper, overhead transparencies, or page protectors, and the appropriate markers. Partners draw their own line on a coordinate plane that passes through the origin. Using this line, students explore the following questions:

- What right triangles can you find under your line? Draw as many as you can see.
- How can you describe each triangle?
- What do your triangles have in common? How do you know?
- How could you use your right triangles to predict points on your line that you cannot see?

Partners test the patterns they've found, this time with a new line on the coordinate plane. Encourage students to try lines that are very different from the first one they drew. Using this new line, students explore the questions, Are all the patterns you found still true? Why or why not?

Discuss

As a class, discuss the following questions:

- How did you find different right triangles under your line? (Invite students to share the different ways they found or saw triangles under a line, where the line is the hypotenuse.)
- What did your triangles have in common? How do you know? (Invite students to share their triangles on the document camera and their evidence for similarity.)
- How did you look for connections between these triangles? What strategies did you use?
- Will right triangles under a line on the coordinate plane always be similar or in proportion? Why or why not?

In this discussion, focus on the lengths of the legs of the right triangles students formed and how students can iterate these to form new triangles and similar triangles. These legs form the rise and run of the slope of the line.

Look-Fors

- **Are students making only congruent triangles?** Students may identify a single right triangle under the line and then proceed to iterate that triangle in a string, up and down the line. This is certainly a useful finding—that no matter what the position, the same triangle can be formed under the line. However, if students stick with this single way of seeing right triangles under the line, they may conclude that all the right triangles that can be formed are congruent. If you notice partners stuck in this way of thinking, ask, Are there any other right triangles possible? It is hoped that in the launch, students saw different sizes of triangles, and you can refer groups back to that image to ask, Can you make triangles larger or smaller than the ones you've made?
- **Are students only looking for triangles with integer coordinates, or are they exploring between the integer coordinates and considering rational values for the vertices?** It is natural that students will look for points where

their line intersects with whole-number units on the grid. These points are easier to describe and count with confidence and precision. However, the patterns of similarity are infinitely scalable. Eighth graders need more opportunities to reason with and see rational numbers, seeing the continuous nature of number. Look for opportunities to push students to consider triangles that fall between these whole-number units. For instance, if students find a triangle 3 units long and 2 units high (the smallest whole-number triangle possible, in this case), you could press them to find an even smaller triangle. Some students might try this on their own, and if you notice this, be sure to ask them how they are reasoning about the size of the triangle. Be sure that students who have considered rational-number coordinates or side lengths share their findings with the class in the discussion.

Reflect

If you know the shape of a right triangle that can be made under a line, can you draw the line? Why or why not? Use an example to explain your thinking.

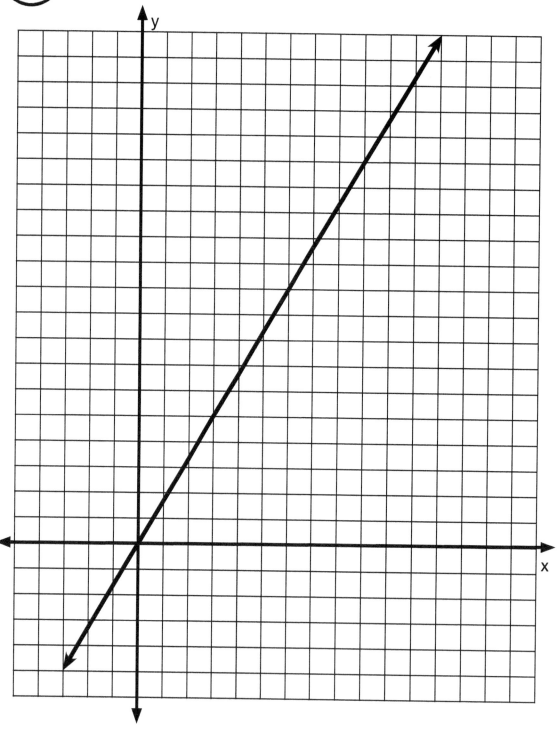

Stairway to Eleven

Snapshot

Students investigate slope by designing a staircase with a railing, connecting parallel lines on the coordinate plane to slope.

Connection to CCSS
8.EE.5, 8.EE.6, 8.EE.8b

Agenda

Activity	Time	Description/Prompt	Materials
Launch	5–10 min	Show students the Staring at Staircases sheet and discuss what makes these staircases different from each other. Draw attention to differences in steepness, slope, or the rise and run of the stairs. Tell students that they will be designing their own staircase today.	Staring at Staircases sheet, to display
Explore	30–40 min	Groups design a staircase that spans 11 vertical feet. Students consider the height (rise) and tread length (run) of each stair, the slope of the staircase overall, and its horizontal distance. Groups plot their staircases on a coordinate plane, add a railing, and determine where this railing intersects with the *y*-axis. Students consider what other designs could and could not work.	• Make available tools for constructing staircases: snap cubes, blocks, square tiles, yardsticks or meter sticks, masking or painters tape, or yarn • Make available tools for recording: grid paper (see appendix), colors, and rulers

Activity	Time	Description/Prompt	Materials
Discuss	20 min	Discuss how groups made decisions about their designs, including the rise and run of the stairs. Groups share their designs, the slopes they used, and their reasoning about the railing. Connect parallel lines and equal slope. Discuss the properties of staircases that do not work.	
Extend	40+ min	Take students to places where they can walk real staircases with varying slopes. Students explore what it feels to climb stairs of different slopes. Students compare the slopes of real staircases to those they designed and make revisions to their designs based on how they think their staircases would feel.	• Access to multiple staircases • Measurement tools, such as rulers, meter sticks, or yardsticks

To the Teacher

We've designed this activity so that it begins with examining and comparing photos of staircases, with the goal of giving students a way to see that staircases do not all have the same steepness. However, it may be more compelling to physically investigate staircases in your school and community first, so that instead of *seeing* that staircases are different, students can *feel* those differences in their bodies. We've placed this idea in the extension, because we know that not all schools have staircases. However, if your school does have stairs of different slopes, you may want to introduce this investigation by having students experience the differences in slope and asking them what makes a staircase too steep or too shallow. They can use exploration in the real world to help them design their own stairs and make the case for what defines a safe slope.

Activity

Launch

Launch the activity by showing students the Staring at Staircases sheet on the document camera. Ask, What makes these staircases different from each other? Give students a chance to turn and talk to a partner. Take some observations about differences. Be sure to focus students' attention on the difference in the rise, run, slope, or steepness, however students might describe these features, and notice that stairs can be steeper or shallower.

Tell students that they are going to design a set of stairs to go from one story to another, and they will need to consider how steep the stairs should be.

Explore

Make available tools for building stairs (such as snap cubes, blocks, square tiles, yardsticks or meter sticks, masking or painters tape, or yarn) and tools for designing and recording (such as grid paper [see appendix], colors, and rulers).

Groups work together to design a staircase to go from one floor to the next, spanning a vertical distance of 11 feet. The following questions guide students' work:

- How high should a stair be? Why?
- How long should the tread be? Why?
- What is the slope of your staircase? Why?
- How do you know your staircase is not too shallow or too steep?
- How long will your staircase be horizontally?

Groups then put their design for the staircase on a coordinate plane, where the floor is at the origin. Students add a railing to their staircase, considering the following questions:

- How could you represent the railing on the graph of your stairs?
- Where would your railing cross the y-axis? (i.e., What is the railing's y-intercept?)

Encourage students to consider alternate solutions to the staircase design:

- Could you have made a different staircase? What other designs could work for this task?
- What designs would not have worked? Why?

Discuss

Before groups share their specific designs, discuss the ways in which students tackled decision making through the following questions:

- What are some of the things you thought about in designing your stairs? Why?
- Why did you choose the length of tread you did?
- Why did you choose the height of the step you did?
- How did you know your stairs were not too steep or too shallow?
- What was challenging about designing your staircase? Why?

Invite groups to share their different designs:

- What slope did you use? How did you find the slope of your stairs?
- How do our different designs for the staircase compare?
- How can we use our different designs to decide what is too steep? Too shallow?
- What did you notice about the railing for your stairs? Where did it cross the *y*-axis? What does this mean?
- What designs will not work for an 11-foot staircase? Why?

Use this discussion to connect the specific rise (height) and run (length) of each stair to the slope of the staircase, and to show how the stairs and railing have the same slope, even though one is a line (railing) and one is stepped. Point out that having the same slope makes the two lines parallel, something important for a railing on a staircase.

Extend

If you have stairs available in your school or community, compare the slope of the existing stairs to that of the staircase each group designed. Try to give students experiences with stairs that are steeper and shallower so that they can feel in their bodies what effect different slopes can have. Consider different contexts for stairs beyond full interior staircases, such as bleachers, porches, garden walkways, stages or auditoriums, or playgrounds. Students could collect data in their own homes or neighborhoods to expand their data set. Provide students with measurement tools such as rulers, meter sticks, or yardsticks. Using these additional examples of staircases, students explore the following questions:

- How do the slopes of different staircases compare to the one your group designed?
- How do the stairs in your world feel when you're climbing them?
- How do you expect the stairs you designed would feel?
- What revisions would you make to your design based on exploring real stairs? Why?

Look-Fors

- **Are students designing stairs with a consistent slope?** One feature of staircases is that, although one staircase may be different from another, each is internally consistent. Each stair within a staircase should have the same tread length and rise, creating a consistent slope. This is true even if students design a staircase with a landing; each portion of the staircase should be internally consistent and have the same slope as the other portions. If you notice variation, ask students about their thinking with such questions as, How did you decide on the height and tread length of each stair? Why are the stairs different? How do you think that would feel to climb? If students are genuinely confused about the need for the same slope, you might look for opportunities for them to examine a real set of stairs in your school building, or return to the Staring at Staircases sheet to ask them how people who design stairs deal with this question. Is each stair designed individually, or is a rule used?

- **Are students' staircase designs realistic?** Students may struggle to know what an appropriate stair height or tread length is. Ask, How could you use your bodies and your memories of climbing stairs to help you? How long is a tread in relationship to your foot? How high do you have to lift your leg to climb? Students may not know these answers as quantities, but they hold knowledge of them in their bodies. Students may want to model their stairs in real (rather than proportional) lengths using masking tape or yarn on a wall so that they can estimate how far they need to lift a foot or how big a stair needs to be to comfortably balance.

- **Are students connecting slope, stairs, and the right triangle formed under the line?** At this point students have had many experiences with looking for right triangles under a line and connecting these to the idea of slope. Staircases create a physical representation of those triangles; it is the line that is implied. In this investigation, look for opportunities to connect the line, its slope, the triangle underneath it, and its rise and run. Each of these components has a real physical and practical meaning in this context. Be sure to notice ways that students are making these connections and highlight them in the closing discussion.

- **How are students plotting their staircase onto the coordinate plane?** When groups move their design to a coordinate plane, they will need to consider how to represent their design proportionally. Ask questions about how they will scale their axes so that the full length and height of the staircase can be shown. Ask, What units will make it easiest to plot the individual stairs? Choosing increments intentionally will make drawing the staircase and, ultimately, adding a railing, far easier.

Reflect

How do you think slopes are related to angles?

BIG IDEA **4**

Comparing Patterns of Growth

A few years ago, I taught my first summer school, working with a group of students in a local school district who had been referred to a summer math class by their teachers. Most of the students, not surprisingly, did not want to be there that summer, and they communicated that on the first day, sitting hunched over the desks with their hoods up, either quietly resistant or more loudly disruptive. We worked together on tasks similar to those in this book, and within days the classroom environment was transformed. Every morning, students would jostle at the door to get into the room and continue their mathematical explorations.

I remember clearly one of the activities we gave the students; it was similar to the Play activity in this big idea. The students were given an 8 × 8 chessboard image and asked how many squares they could find. The students enthusiastically began searching for squares, but then something unexpected happened. The students' results differed markedly, with some students finding cool patterns of numbers and some not, and I quickly realized that the difference was that the students who were finding patterns had been able to organize their results well. In addition, the differing achievements of the students matched their prior achievement, with the high achievers organizing well and the low achievers failing to do so. The students were able to find lots of different-size squares, but they had not learned to organize their findings. This was fascinating to me, and I realized in those moments that the previously low-achieving students needed to learn how to organize their work. Any mathematical investigation, and I could argue any mathematical thought, requires organization, and the task we gave our students of finding and recording squares highlighted this mathematical practice. We spent time that summer teaching the students how to organize their results, using tables and other representations, which meant that their problem-solving and pattern-seeking capabilities increased dramatically.

In our Visualize activity, students are shown a 3 × 3 square made up of smaller squares, and asked to work out the number of squares, in a number talk forum. They are then given squares of their own to investigate. A method that really helps with organization is color-coding, and we recommend its use in this activity. Students can use color to highlight patterns in the charts and tables they produce. With each new case we give students, there is a new square size to be tracked, making organization really important.

Our Play activity invites students to see number patterns in a skip-counting array. We ask students to start with a number and skip-count up so that they generate a whole table of numbers, then to freely search for their own patterns. Our Youcubed team has started to explore skip-counting arrays ourselves, and we have become fascinated by the different patterns we have found. We envisage students having rich discussions about the patterns they uncover, what they mean, and how they relate to other mathematical ideas such as algebra.

Our Investigate activity is one that Cathy Williams created and has been using with groups of teachers and students, with amazing results. The idea of systems of linear equations is an important one in eighth-grade. This activity provides an ideal need for this kind of thinking and can be the occasion for students learning to use these systems. But the openness of the task means that there are many directions in which students can go, and different answers may emerge, which is something I always love, as I can remind students that mathematics problems do not always have one solution. Part of the complexity of the activity is understanding what the problem is asking—it takes careful reading and thinking. This is good, as too few mathematics problems encourage or need this kind of careful reading, thinking, and interpreting. Once students understand what the problem is asking, you can give them the freedom to approach the question in any way they wish—with true mathematical freedom.

Jo Boaler

Squared Squares

Snapshot

Students investigate and compare patterns of change in square grids.

Connection to CCSS
8.F.2, 8.EE.5

Agenda

Activity	Time	Description/Prompt	Materials
Launch	10–15 min	Show students the 3 × 3 Square sheet and facilitate a number talk about how many squares students see. Come to agreement that there are squares of different sizes and that there is a total of 14 squares. Tell students that this is case 3 of a pattern that they will be exploring today.	3 × 3 Square sheet, to display
Explore	40 min	Partners investigate the number of squares of each size contained within each case of the grid square pattern. Students explore how the number of each size of square grows from case to case, and create a visual proof comparing the patterns of growth they find.	• Grid paper (see appendix), colors, and chart paper, per partnership • Make available: square tiles, patty paper, scissors, and tape
Discuss	20 min	Students post their visual proofs and do a gallery walk to compare. As a class, talk about the different ways that students displayed their findings visually. Discuss the patterns of growth that students found and how they compare.	

Activity	Time	Description/Prompt	Materials
Extend	40+ min	Partners design a series of growing similar rectangles and investigate the number and size of squares contained in each case of their pattern. Students compare patterns of growth among the sizes of squares from case to case and explore whether these patterns are the same as or different from those in the earlier square pattern.	Grid paper (see appendix), colors, and square tiles, for each partnership

To the Teacher

In this activity, we invite students to compare patterns of growth embedded in a series of squares. Talking about these patterns can be challenging because we are examining squares inside of squares, and this creates a need to be precise with language for clarity. We present students first with case 3 of a growing square pattern, and we ask students how many squares are inside of this 3 × 3 square. We encourage you to take a moment yourself to try to count the squares of different sizes it contains.

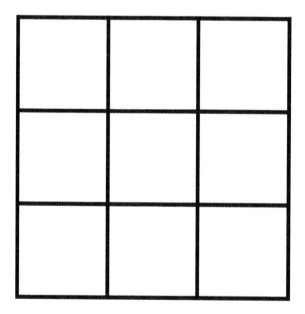

Counting squares in a 3 × 3 square produces nine 1 × 1 squares, four 2 × 2 squares, and one 3 × 3 square, for a total of 14 squares.

We find that students often struggle to see the squares of different sizes that the gridded squares contain. Here there are nine 1 × 1 squares, four 2 × 2 squares, and one 3 × 3 square, for a total of 14 squares. Before students can investigate how the number of each of these different sizes of squares changes from case to case, they need to be able to see and count the squares.

Once students are clear on what we are counting in this activity, there are two major challenges they will face. First, partners need to develop ways of organizing data to be able to look for patterns. This is particularly challenging because they need to track several different kinds of patterns, including how the number of 1 × 1 squares grows from case to case, how the number of 2 × 2 squares grows, and so on. With every new case, there is a new square size to be tracked. Students will need ways to organize this data, which could include tables, graphs, and color-coding.

Second, once students have some data organized, they need to think about the patterns of growth and how they compare. That is, how does the number of 1 × 1 squares grow? How does that pattern of growth compare with the way the number of 2 × 2 squares grows? We were intrigued by this puzzle ourselves and were interested to see that the number of squares of each size grows in precisely the same way; it is just that the starting points of these patterns are offset. That is, 1 × 1 squares begin to grow in case 1, but 2 × 2 squares don't appear until case 2, and so on. The pattern for how these square grow is exponential, counting up by squares of whole numbers: 1, 4, 9, 16, and so on.

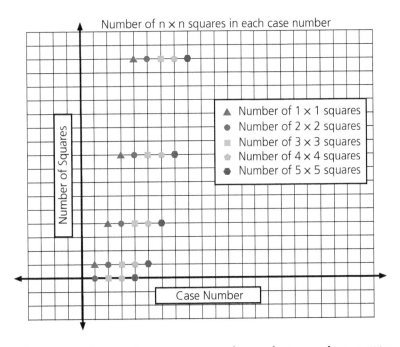

The number of squares in each case grows in an interesting pattern of curves.

Activity

Launch

Launch the activity by showing students the 3 × 3 Square sheet on the document camera. Ask, How many squares do you see? Facilitate this like a number talk, giving students a chance to think first and then taking student responses. Ask students to defend their answers until the class can agree that there are squares of different sizes and that there is a total of 14.

Tell students that this 3 × 3 square represents case 3 of a pattern and that they are going explore the integer cases of this pattern. Tell students that we want to know how the number of squares of different sizes (1 × 1, 2 × 2, . . .) grows from case to case.

Explore

Provide partners with grid paper (see appendix), colors, and chart paper. Make available square tiles and patty paper for students who want to build or fold grid squares, and scissors and tape for students to mount their patterns on chart paper. Partners investigate the following questions:

- How many squares do you see in a 2 × 2 (case 2), 3 × 3 (case 3), or 4 × 4 (case 4) grid square?
- How can you count the squares? What sizes are there? How many squares of each size are there?
- What patterns are there in the number of squares and their sizes?
- What happens when the case number gets larger or smaller? How does the number of squares grow across cases?
- Do the different-size squares grow at the same rates? Why or why not?
- How could you show these patterns of growth?

Partners construct a visual proof of their findings. Encourage students to create visualizations and justifications of the patterns of growth they found.

Discuss

Invite students to post their visual proofs around the room and then do a gallery walk during which students examine and compare the patterns that groups found and the ways they made these patterns visible.

As a class, discuss the following questions:

- How did you organize your data to look for patterns?
- What patterns did you find?
- How does the number of squares of different sizes grow from case to case? Do they grow at the same rate? Why or why not?
- What mistakes did you make? What was challenging? Why?

Highlight interesting ways that students developed to show and compare the patterns of growth. Visualizing patterns is challenging work. Notice graphs, tables, or other displays that make it easier to see growth and compare across the data.

Extend

Partners design their own series of similar growing rectangles. For instance, they could design a series that begins with 1×2, 2×4, 3×6, ... This is a series of similar rectangles because, in each case, one side is double the other. Using the series they have created, partners explore the following questions:

- What squares can you find inside your series? How many squares can you find inside each case in your series?
- How does the number of different sizes of squares grow from case to case?
- How do these patterns of growth compare with the growing squares series? Why might they be different?
- What other questions do these patterns raise for you?
- What other dimensions of your series could you compare (for example, changes in the area versus changes in perimeter)?

Provide partners tools for designing and exploring squares in rectangular patterns, including grid paper (see appendix), colors, and square tiles.

Look-Fors

- **Are students clear about what they are counting?** One of the goals of the number talk in the launch is to come to shared understanding about what is being counted inside the grid squares. Students need to develop systems for counting so that they can ensure that they have counted all of the 1×1, 2×2, 3×3, and larger squares. Ask students, How are you counting the squares?

How can you be sure you've counted all the squares of one size? Thinking systematically is key, but not obvious to all students. Support them in decomposing this task into parts so that they can develop counting systems.

- **Are students' ways of organizing their data going to support looking for patterns of growth?** There are many ways that students might record their findings, and some will support looking for patterns of growth better than others. For instance, if students simply make lists for each case square (such as "Case 3: 9 1 × 1, 4 2 × 2, 1 3 × 3"), they will likely find it hard to look across the cases for patterns. Tables and graphs will make seeing patterns easier. You might also ask students how color could help them keep track of the numbers that are associated with different sizes of squares. You might point out the ways that students are organizing and ask, How could this way help you see patterns? Is there any other way you could organize that would make seeing patterns easier? What ways could you try?

- **Are students making comparisons between patterns of growth?** In the process of analyzing patterns of growth to understand each pattern individually, students may lose track of making comparisons. For some students, the observation that each size of square grows in the same way may jump out at them, particularly if they have organized their data in a way that makes this visible. Others, however, may benefit from being asked explicitly about comparing the patterns of growth. You might ask, How does the pattern of growth of 1 × 1 squares compare to the pattern of growth of 2 × 2 or any other size square? Be sure to probe students in their groups as to why they think these might be the same. Get students interested in why the number of squares of different sizes inside squares grows at the same rate and why that rate is a squared pattern (x^2).

Reflect

How can you tell when two patterns of change are the same or different?

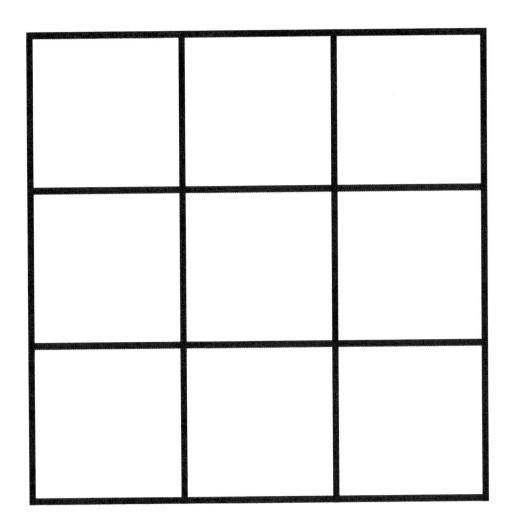

Skip-Counting Arrays

Snapshot

Students explore and compare integer patterns embedded in skip-counting arrays, making connection to systems of linear equations.

Connection to CCSS
8.EE.5, 8.EE.7a, 8.EE.8, 8.F.4

Agenda

Activity	Time	Description/Prompt	Materials
Launch	10 min	Show students the Skip-Counting Array sheet and ask them what patterns they see. Color-code the different patterns that students observe.	• Skip-Counting Array sheet, to display • Colors
Play	30+ min	Partners first explore the patterns they can find, describe, and compare in the Skip-Counting Array sheet. Then they create their own skip-counting arrays to explore. Students look for, describe, and compare patterns embedded in different kinds of arrays.	• Skip-Counting Array sheet, per partnership • Colors, per partnership
Discuss	15–20 min	Discuss the differences and similarities in the patterns students found in the Skip-Counting Array. Discuss what might be the sources of these patterns. Invite students to share the different skip-counting arrays they created and the patterns they found within. Support students in comparing patterns and thinking about the sources of similarities and differences.	

To the Teacher

In this activity, we invite students to play with what we are calling *skip-counting arrays*. A skip-counting array can be made by choosing an integer value for skip-counting, and recording it, beginning at any value, in an array with a predetermined number of columns. Some incredible patterns emerge when you try this. Since we've started exploring skip-counting arrays ourselves, we've become fascinated by all the patterns they can contain. We start here by exploring a skip-counting array made by skip-counting by 3s beginning at −12 and arranging the sequence in five columns. In this array, you can see several patterns, such as the following:

- Moving down a column (vertically) adds 15 to each value (or conversely, moving up a column subtracts 15).
- Moving across a row (horizontally) adds/subtracts 3 to get the next value.
- Moving on a diagonal with a negative slope adds 18; the diagonal with the positive slope adds 12.
- Numbers alternate even and odd. Other alternating patterns can be seen in each vertical column, where the ones digits alternate.
- Moving diagonally one space down and two spaces to the right adds 21.

Each pattern of movement generates a different pattern of change, regardless of the starting point. These arrays connect with linear patterns and systems of equations. Each has an intercept along the left side and a slope or rate of change. We encourage you to use this language when talking about patterns of movement. Where two patterns intersect, we see an example of a solution to a system of linear equations. We encourage you to try these arrays yourself and see how the patterns change when you alter the skip-count value, the start value, and the number of columns.

Consider developing a space to display the patterns students find in their different skip-counting arrays. Invite students to point out conjectures, questions, and wonders that arise out of these patterns. Encourage students to continue to explore these patterns and the questions they generate by adding findings to this display space.

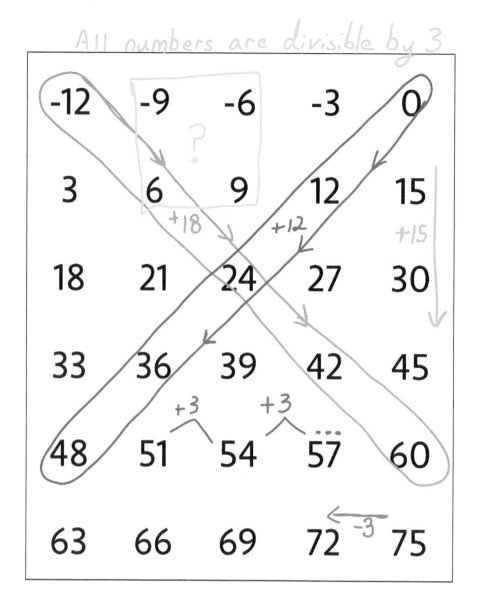

All numbers are divisible by 3

An example of color-coded notations showing patterns found in the skip-counting array

Activity

Launch

Launch the activity by showing students the Skip-Counting Array sheet. Tell students simply that this is a pattern of numbers. Ask, What patterns do you see? Give students a chance to turn and talk to a partner. Then invite students to come up and point out patterns. Mark and label each pattern with a different color. You do not want this sharing to become exhaustive; however, you do want students to see more than the core pattern of skip-counting by 3s. Looking across the rows as we might read a page of text is only one way of looking for patterns. Be sure that students see that there are other ways before they head off to work more with this pattern.

Play

Provide partners with the Skip-Counting Array sheet and colors. Students build on the patterns observed by the class in exploring the following questions:

- What patterns do you see? Extend the array as far as you'd like. Record the patterns you observe on the sheet.
- How can these patterns be described generally? (For instance, with words, numbers, symbols, and/or color-coding)
- Why are the patterns different?

Partners then design their own skip-counting array to explore how the patterns change. Encourage students to play with different skip-counting values and different table widths. Partners look for patterns in their array, describe each one, and compare them.

- If you extend your array, do the patterns you've observed continue? Why or why not?
- What happens to the patterns you've noticed if you change the number of columns in your table? Why?
- What does it mean when two patterns intersect?
- How are the patterns you've found different? Why? What creates differences in patterns that run horizontally, vertically, and diagonally?
- When are patterns the same? Why?

Partners might explore these questions with multiple skip-counting arrays.

Discuss

Begin by discussing the original skip-counting array:

- What patterns did you find? (Color-code the patterns students identify.)
- How can you describe the patterns you found? (Label the different patterns using words, numbers, and symbols.)
- How can one sequence generate so many different patterns? What creates these different patterns?

Invite students to share the skip-counting arrays they made and discuss the following questions:

- What patterns did you find?
- What does it mean when two pattern intersect?
- How do the skip-counting interval and the number of columns change the patterns you find?
- How do the patterns change when you extend them into negative integers?

In both discussions, draw attention to the ways that patterns of change compare, and how differences and similarities are connected to the pathways the patterns follow on the array. That is, any two vertical patterns on the same array will have the same pattern, but they will be different from any diagonal pattern. When discussing patterns that intersect, be sure to draw attention to the idea that the intersection value is part of both patterns. This observation plants the seed for the idea of simultaneous solutions to systems of linear equations.

Look-Fors

- **Are students looking for creative patterns?** Push students to look for more complex patterns and those that might not seem obvious. For instance, students may stop with horizontal, vertical, and diagonal patterns. Ask, What other ways could you move on the array? If you made your array wider (increased the number of columns), what new kinds of movement could you try? Also, students may notice patterns not strictly associated with rates of change, such as those connected with repeating digits, even and odd numbers, or symmetry around zero. Although these connections to linear equations are not as clear, encourage all kinds of pattern seeking so that students stay open to the vast diversity of patterns possible.
- **Are students thinking about the reasoning behind similarities and differences among patterns?** In all the pattern hunting, be sure to ask students to think about the differences and similarities between the patterns they have found and why these might be so. For instance, why are the vertical patterns always the same no matter where you start? Why is it that these vertical patterns do change, though, if you alter the skip-counting value or the number

of columns? Why are the patterns of change in the two diagonal directions different? Press students to think about what is happening inside the skip-counting array that leads to these different kinds of patterns.

- **Do any students make connections with linear equations or rates of change?** Listen for students drawing on their knowledge of linear change to describe the patterns they see. Students may use linear change ideas (such as, "The change is the same each time you move down one") or language (such as *rate of change, slope, line,* or *linear*). If you hear this kind of reasoning, ask probing questions that draw out these connections. You might ask, How is this like a linear pattern? or How can you see the rate of change here? Is there a way you could graph these patterns? What might they look like? Be sure to highlight these connections in the closing discussion.

Reflect

What creates different patterns in skip-counting arrays?

−12   −9   −6   −3   0

3   6   9   12   15

18   21   24   27   30

33   36   39   42   45

48   51   54   57   60

63   66   69   72   75

Stacking Pennies

Snapshot

Students investigate the proportional relationships involved in making a dollar from equal groups of pennies, which can be represented with linear equations.

Connection to CCSS
8.EE.8, 8.F.1., 8.F.2, 8.F.4

Agenda

Activity	Time	Description/Prompt	Materials
Launch	10 min	Show students the Stacking Pennies sheet and ask them what numbers are represented in the visuals and what patterns they notice in these numbers. Discuss the constraints of the task.	• Stacking Pennies sheet, to display • Optional: pennies
Explore	30+ min	Provide students the Stacking Pennies sheet. Partners work together to find solutions in which the stacks of pennies on the number visuals for 3, 5, 6, 7, and 9 sum to $1.00 and satisfy the constraints. Students work to generate and organize data to look for patterns and solutions. Partners create a chart to display their findings.	• Stacking Pennies sheet, per partnership • Chart paper and colors, per partnership • Make available: grid paper (see appendix), hundred chart, and tape
Discuss	20+ min	Partners post their charts and do a gallery walk, noticing the strategies groups used. Discuss students' findings, including the relationships they found, the strategies used, and how they organized their data. Develop ideas about how many solutions might exist and how one could find them all.	

Activity	Time	Description/Prompt	Materials
Extend	40+ min	Invite partners to create their own Stacking Pennies task by making modifications to the numbers involved. Students then try to generate solutions to their task and compare the results to those from the original task.	• Number Visuals sheet, per partnership • Make available: grid paper (see appendix), hundred charts, and colors

To the Teacher

In this activity, we ask students to find a solution to a problem that has many solutions. The parameters of this task can be challenging to understand at first, and we encourage you to spend time supporting students in making sense of them. The key is for students to understand that the stacks of pennies within a single number visual all must have the same number of pennies. That is, you must make three equal-height stacks on the number 3, and five equal-height stacks on the number 5, and so on. But the stacks on different numbers do not need to be equal. For instance, the stacks on the number 3 could each be four pennies high, for a total of 12 pennies, while the stacks on the number 5 could be two pennies high, for a total of 10 pennies.

The central mathematical ideas in this activity are proportional reasoning and linear relationships. Students may recognize that the number of possible pennies on each number visual aligns with the multiples of that number. That is, the total number of pennies that can be arranged on the number 3 can only be 3, 6, 9, 12, 15, and so on. The number of pennies is in proportion to the number they rest on. Students may also try representing these relationships symbolically. For instance, students may think of this task as follows:

$$3a + 5b + 6c + 7d + 9e = 100$$

Although this equation does not present any ready solutions, it stretches what is possible for symbolic representation beyond two variables. Alternatively, students might think of the relationships as a series of linear equations, each of which yields the number of pennies on a single number visual, such as:

$$y = 3x$$
$$y = 5x$$
$$y = 6x$$
$$y = 7x$$
$$y = 9x$$

These individual equations can lead to a graphical approach for seeing the total numbers of pennies possible on each number visual, as can be seen in the photo on the left. The same idea could be represented on a hundred chart (shown in the center), in which the number of possible pennies is color-coded by number. That is, for the number 3, the possible numbers of pennies (3, 6, 9, and so on) are marked with a black dot, just as they are on the graph. Other students may generate organized lists to connect combinations that sum to 100, such as in the image on the right. Your students will likely come up with other ways of generating possibilities and coordinating them into solutions.

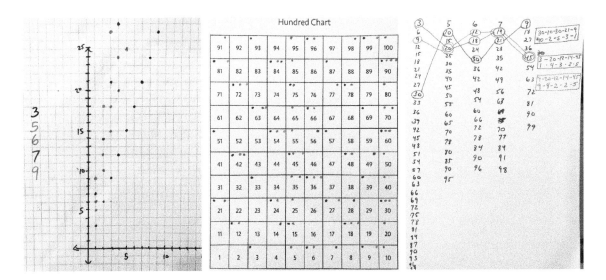

Student work examples showing creative ways to make sense
of the Stacking Pennies problem.

Activity

Launch

Launch the activity by showing students the Stacking Pennies sheet on the document camera. Ask students, What numbers are represented by these images? What patterns do you notice in these numbers? Give students a chance to turn and talk to a partner about the number visuals. Discuss what students noticed, and be sure to label the five number visuals as representing the numbers 3, 5, 6, 7, and 9.

Ask students to read the constraints and the central question at the bottom of the Stacking Pennies sheet. Ask, What does this mean? Give students a chance to turn and talk to a partner about how they are interpreting this task. Discuss the constraints and the question as a group. Be sure that students understand that within a number, the stacks must be the same size, but each number may have different sizes of stacks. Tell students that no number can have zero coins. You may want to invite students to come up to the document camera to model these constraints using coins on the Stacking Pennies sheet.

Explore

Provide partners with the Stacking Pennies sheet, chart paper, and colors. Make available grid paper (see appendix), hundred charts, and tape. As shown on the Stacking Pennies sheet, partners are asked to imagine that each of the number visuals for 3, 5, 6, 7, and 9 is stacked with pennies such that total of the stacks is $1.00. The stacks of pennies within each number must be of equal size or height, but each number can have different-size stacks. No number can have zero pennies. Partners explore the following questions:

- What could be the size of the stacks of pennies in each number visual, if the sum of the pennies is $1.00?
- How many solutions can you find?
- How can you organize your thinking to help you look for solutions?
- What patterns do you see that can help you look for solutions?
- How can you display your findings? Make a chart that shows how you found your solutions.

Encourage students to create innovative ways of generating and organizing data that can help them as they search for solutions, including using graphs, lists, hundred charts, and color-coding.

Discuss

Post students' charts and do a gallery walk. As students walk, ask them to notice the different strategies groups used for organizing and searching for solutions.

Discuss students' findings through the following questions:

- What strategies did you use to look for a solution? How did you deal with all the constraints?
- How did you organize your data to make sense of the possibilities?
- What patterns did you notice that helped you look for solutions?
- What solutions did you find? How did you know you had found a solution that fits all the constraints?

- Are there any patterns to the solutions?
- How many solutions do you think there are? Why? How could you go about trying to find them all?

Extend

Invite partners to create and attempt to solve their own version of the Stacking Pennies task. Provide students with the Number Visuals sheet and make available colors, grid paper (see appendix), and hundred charts. Partners could choose to modify this task in one or more of the following ways:

- Change the sum of the pennies to a different value—for instance, 50 cents or $2.00.
- Change how many numbers are used. In this task, we used 3, 5, 6, 7, and 9. Students might eliminate one or more of these, or add other numbers.
- Change which numbers are used. For instance, students could use the number visuals for 2, 3, 5, 10, and 11.

Partners define their new, adapted task and then work to find solutions. Encourage students to use what they learned about organizing data in the first task and the gallery walk to develop strategies for solving their own Stacking Pennies task. Partners explore the following questions:

- How did the changes you made to the task change the strategies you used to find solutions?
- How did these changes affect how difficult it was to find solutions?
- How many solutions do you think there are to this task? Do you think there are more or fewer than for the original task? Why?

Look-Fors

- **Are students organizing the data they collect?** This task requires coordinating many different pieces of data across five different patterns. Look for the ways that students are trying to organize all of the possible numbers of pennies on each number visual. You might notice organized lists, graphs, or marked-up hundred charts. If you notice that students are not organizing to look for patterns, and are instead just trying solutions through guess and check, ask questions to help students move toward more systematic approaches. You might ask, How many coins could be on each number visual? How could you organize this data? How could you use this data to search for sums of 100 pennies?

- **What patterns are students finding in their data?** There are several patterns that students might notice and use to support looking for solutions. For instance, this task includes three values that are multiples of 3: 3, 6, and 9. The sum of the pennies on these three numbers will always be a multiple of 3. Students might use this to begin with a large multiple of 3 and decompose it into groups of pennies for each of the numbers 3, 6, and 9. This strategy means that students then only need to tackle finding a multiple of 5 and a multiple of 7 that can complete the sum of 100. Students may also be paying attention to the values in the ones place, knowing that these must sum to 10 or a multiple of 10.

- **How are students thinking about the number of solutions this problem has? Is the number of solutions finite or infinite?** As students develop strategies for searching for solutions, they will begin to find multiple ways to meet the constraints. In fact, there are hundreds of solutions to this task, a number so large that it can feel as though there are infinite solutions, as your class will not come close to finding them all in one or two class periods. However, the number of solutions, though large, is finite. The key question is, How can we tell when the number of solutions is finite or infinite? Encourage students to think about this question in light of the constraints for this task. If your students do the extension activity, this could be a place to explore how changes in constraints might affect the number of solutions, which could shed light on whether the original task has a finite or infinite number of solutions. We encourage you to leave this as an open question that students can continue to explore and debate.

Reflect

How did the patterns you found in this task connect to those in the skip-counting arrays from the Play activity? Draw an example to illustrate one or more connections you noticed.

Stacking Pennies

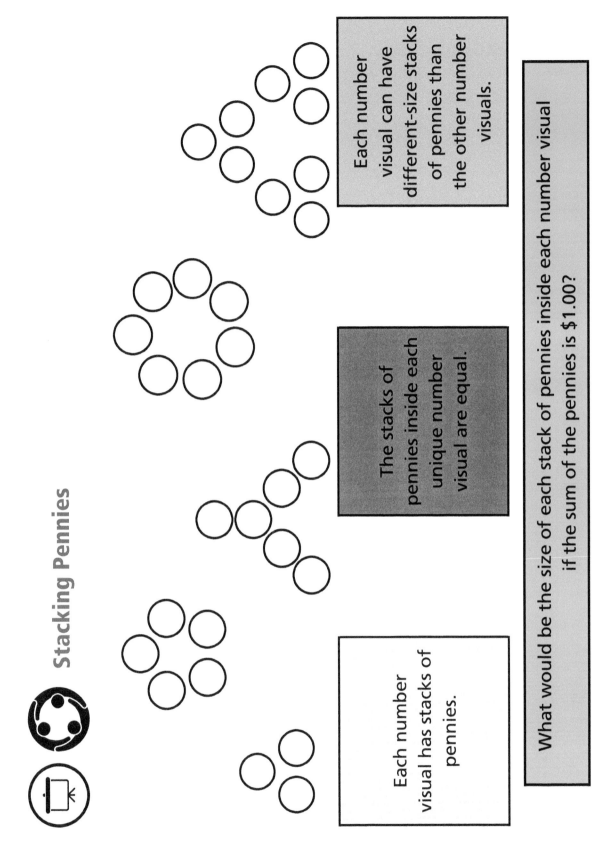

Each number visual can have different-size stacks of pennies than the other number visuals.

The stacks of pennies inside each unique number visual are equal.

Each number visual has stacks of pennies.

What would be the size of each stack of pennies inside each number visual if the sum of the pennies is $1.00?

Hundred Chart

91	92	93	94	95	96	97	98	99	100
81	82	83	84	85	86	87	88	89	90
71	72	73	74	75	76	77	78	79	80
61	62	63	64	65	66	67	68	69	70
51	52	53	54	55	56	57	58	59	60
41	42	43	44	45	46	47	48	49	50
31	32	33	34	35	36	37	38	39	40
21	22	23	24	25	26	27	28	29	30
11	12	13	14	15	16	17	18	19	20
1	2	3	4	5	6	7	8	9	10

Number Visuals

The Ins and Outs of Functions

Why are functions and algebra meaningless to so many students? How did functions, which offer insights into real-world relationships, become a set of rules to remember? US textbooks have led many students, and teachers, astray by introducing algebra and variables to students as a requirement to solve for x. This goes against the research base on algebra in a fundamental way. When we teach students to solve for x, the variable x typically has one solution. But the meaning and essence of variables is that they vary—that they are there to represent a situation that can change. When we show students growing patterns, the case number represents variable, and the case number changes with each case. If students learn that variables can vary, they can later meet situations when the variable has one solution, and this does not provide conflict for them. But when we teach students to solve for x and then ask them to work with situations where the x varies, they become very confused, and some meet a serious conceptual block. This has an easy solution—introduce algebra to students through visual patterns that they can see and understand and represent algebraically.

There is another issue with the "solve for x" approach to algebra in textbooks, one that Cornell mathematician Steve Strogatz (2019) discusses in his book *Infinite Powers*. He describes the algebraic-manipulation approach to mathematics, with variables that are not represented visually, in this way:

> Equations could be massaged almost mindlessly, peacefully; you could add the same term to both sides of an equation, cancel common terms, solve for an unknown quantity, or perform a dozen other procedures and algorithms according to standard recipes. The processes of algebra could be soothingly repetitive, like the pleasures of knitting. But algebra suffered from its emptiness. Its symbols were vacuous. They meant nothing until they were given meaning. There was nothing to visualize. Algebra was left-brained and mechanical. (2019, p. 98)

But what happens when we introduce students to algebra visually? As Strogatz describes, everything changes:

> Equations were no longer sterile; they were now embodiments of sinuous geometric forms. A whole new continent of curves and surfaces opened up as soon as equations were viewed geometrically. Lush jungles of geometric flora and fauna waited to be discovered, cataloged, classified, and dissected. (2019, p. 98)

In this set of activities, we introduce students to the lush jungles that Strogatz describes, deliberately challenging any misconceptions about algebra that students may have developed. They will see functions where the variable varies, and they will be asked to consider noninteger cases, probably for the first time in their lives. They will also explore zero and negative cases. All of these explorations should change students' ideas about algebra.

In our Visualize activity, students are asked to visualize, recognize, and extend visual patterns. They are invited to draw different cases as the case number increases and decreases, and they will be asked to represent their functions in four different ways—as graphs, tables, written descriptions, and algebraic expressions. As students engage with ideas in this multidimensional way, their brains will form connections between different pathways, and they will develop strong, connected understandings.

In our Play activity, we introduce an important function for the world—the relationship between Celsius and Fahrenheit. This presents an interesting situation where it makes sense to look at cases that are in multiples of 5; this is because every increase in 5 degrees Celsius yields an increase of 9 degrees Fahrenheit, and the slope of the graph is $\frac{9}{5}$. We ask students to extend the graph in both directions and to think about the cases between the multiples of 5. Ultimately they create a visual for the inverse function, giving them an opportunity to think flexibly.

In our Investigate activity, we introduce a new idea to students, the concept of "near squares." These are numbers that appear in the multiplication table next to the square numbers, representing rectangles where the dimensions are +1 and −1 of the nearby square. Students are given the opportunity to create their own visualizations and look for patterns in the table. For many students, their prior experiences with the multiplication table may have been negative, or even traumatic, if they were made to memorize it. Harvey Mudd mathematician Francis Su describes memorizing the multiplication table as the most meaningless activity possible. Instead of this, we ask students to explore patterns in the table and to engage flexibly with numbers and patterns.

Jo Boaler

Reference

Strogatz, S. (2019). *Infinite powers: How calculus reveals the secrets of the universe* (Advance reading copy). Boston, MA: Houghton Mifflin Harcourt.

Growing Functions

Snapshot

Students visualize and extend linear patterns, which each represent *functions,* and make connections between written descriptions, coordinate graphs, tables of values, visual patterns, and algebraic expressions. Student explore the meaning of *domain* within these functions.

Connection to CCSS
8.F.1, 8.F.2, 8.F.4, 8.F.

Agenda

Activity	Time	Description/Prompt	Materials
Launch	5–10 min	Show students Pattern B on the Task Cards sheet. Ask students how they see the pattern growing. Discuss and color-code students' ways of seeing squares added. Tell students that this pattern extends in both directions. Ask, What do you think case 0 or −1 would look like? Tell students that they will be extending and representing patterns today.	• Task Cards sheet, to display • Colors
Explore	40 min	Partners analyze the patterns on the Task Cards sheet and prepare a visual representation that shows how they see the pattern growing and predicts cases in both directions, what cases −3, 15, and $\frac{1}{2}$ would look like.	• Task Cards sheet, per partnership • Chart and colors, per partnership • Make available: grid paper (see appendix), square tiles, and tape

Activity	Time	Description/Prompt	Materials
Discuss	15 min	Display all of the work and ask students to do a gallery walk. Choose a few to compare and contrast as a class. Discuss the ways that students thought about extending the pattern forward and backward and how they reasoned about case $\frac{1}{2}$. You may choose to introduce the idea of *domain* in this part of the activity to give language to the debates about negative and rational case numbers.	
Explore	30 min	Partners represent each of the four patterns in four different algebraic ways: table, coordinate graph, written description, and algebraic expression.	• Algebra Representation A, B, C, and D sheets, per partnership • Colors
Discuss	10 min	Discuss the different representations students created for each of the four patterns. Name these patterns as *functions*. Discuss how the different representations could be used to find the number of squares in case 15, –3, or $\frac{1}{2}$.	
Extend	40 min	Partners design their own patterns to fit two different constraints, one that increases with case number and one that decreases with case number. Discuss the patterns and representations students produced.	• Make Your Own Function 1 and 2 sheets, per partnership • Colors and square tiles, per partnership

To the Teacher

This activity launches our exploration of functions with recognizing and extending visual patterns. Students have opportunities to explore these patterns before quantifying the number of squares in each case. The goal is to work visually, thinking about how the shape grows or contracts and where students see the squares being added or subtracted.

In the second part of the activity, we ask students to find different representations for the visual patterns they have extended. For each pattern, students will make a table, plot points on a coordinate graph, describe in words how the pattern extends, and make a generalized expression using symbols and numbers for the pattern. In the discussion of this part of the exploration, you'll use these patterns to define a linear *function* as a linear pattern in which each input (case) has exactly one output (number of squares).

We have worked with these kinds of pile patterns in previous grades, but in this activity we introduce the possibility that the patterns are continuous and can extend across the real number system by asking, What does case $\frac{1}{2}$ look like? For these patterns and those you might explore beyond this activity, we encourage you to ask yourself and discuss with students what kind of values bound the pattern. For example, Are there any shapes between the integer case numbers? If so, what would they look like? Is this a continuous function over the set of real numbers? Does it have a domain that includes only the integers? Is the domain infinite over the set of integers, or are there case numbers for only some of the integers? These are questions that have different answers depending on how the students see the pattern change. If students see the pattern ending when there are no more squares, then the pattern has a different domain than if the students see the pattern going on to infinity in both directions.

Activity

Launch

Launch the activity by showing students Pattern B from the Task Cards sheet on the document camera. Ask, How do you see the shapes change as the case number increases? Where do you see the new squares? Give students a chance to turn and talk and then invite students to share the ways they see the pattern growing. Color-code these different ways on the Task Card. If students see the pattern growing in only one way, press them by asking, Is there another way you could see it?

Tell students that this pattern extends in both directions. Ask, What do you think case 0 looks like? Case −1? Give students a chance to turn and talk to generate some thinking. Tell students that today they are going to explore ways to represent this and other patterns visually and with tools that help us extend and generalize.

Explore

Provide partners with the Task Cards sheet, chart paper, and colors. Make available grid paper (see appendix), square tiles, and tape. Partners analyze each of the four patterns on the task cards and prepare a visual representation of the pattern that addresses the following questions:

- How do you see the shapes change as the case number increases?
- Where do you see the new squares?
- How do you see the shapes change as the case number decreases?
- What would case 15 look like?
- What would case −3 look like?
- What would case $\frac{1}{2}$ look like?

As they answer these questions, ask students to make their work clear and detailed so that others can understand their thinking. Color-coding can be used to show how the drawing is connected to the table, graph, writing, and expression.

Discuss

Post students' visual representations around the classroom and do a gallery walk. As students walk, ask them to think about the different ways that students represented the patterns and what differences they notice. If these differences raise debates, be sure to tackle them in this whole-class discussion. Choose a few examples to compare. You might want to focus on different ways of representing the same pattern or on contrasting two different patterns, such as Pattern A and Pattern D.

Discuss the following questions as a class:

- How did you extend each pattern forward to case 15? What did you have to think about?
- How did you extend each pattern backward to case −3? How did you imagine this looking? Why?
- How did you think about case $\frac{1}{2}$?

Some students may not agree and will believe that there are images only for the integer case numbers. Some may think that the case numbers are not infinite. Tell students that the range or types of numbers to which the pattern applies is called the *domain*. Ask, What do you think is the domain of each of these patterns? Why? You can discuss whether or not the domain is over the set of real numbers or over the set of integers.

Explore

Now that students have completed the patterns and seen the different ways that others have recorded their thinking, ask students to represent each pattern algebraically in four ways: with a table of values, a coordinate graph, a written description, and an algebraic expression. Provide students with the Algebra Representations A, B, C, and D sheets, colors, and access to their charts. Partners may choose to complete these representations in any order, and we expect students to struggle with thinking about how to create representations in these different ways.

Discuss

Discuss each of the patterns in turn:

- What could a table of values look like for this pattern? Why?
- What could a coordinate graph look like for this pattern? Why?
- What might a written description of this pattern sound like? Why?
- How could you represent this pattern with an algebraic expression? Are there different ways? Why or why not?

Tell students that each of these patterns is an example of a *function*. A function is a kind of pattern in which each input has exactly one output. Here that means that for each case in the pattern, there is only one number of squares. You might ask, How can you see this idea of one input, one output in your table? Graph? Written description? And expression?

In the first half of this activity, we asked students to project what cases 15, −3, and $\frac{1}{2}$ would look like. After students have generalized these functions, you can have a discussion about how you might have made these predictions using the table, graph, written description, and expressions they've created.

Extend

Provide partners with Make Your Own Function 1 and 2 sheets, colors, and square tiles. Partners make up their own patterns to fit two given constraints. For the first function, we ask students to make a pattern that grows as the case number increases. For the second function, we ask that they make a pattern that gets smaller as the case number increases. For each function students create, they represent it in pictures, in a table, in a coordinate graph, and as an algebraic expression.

When students have completed their patterns and representations, invite students to share the different patterns they have created. Discuss the following questions:

- Are the patterns you made all functions? How do you know?
- Are all of the functions linear? How do you know whether they are linear or not?

Look-Fors

- **How are students reasoning about extending the pattern when the answers are less clear?** For each of the patterns, some of the cases are far easier to envision than others. For instance, students will likely find it logical to extend Pattern B to case 15, where each case as it increases adds a single square to the pattern. As any of the patterns shrink approaching zero, however, students may struggle to imagine how the pattern can extend to something less than zero. Students may similarly struggle with imagining case $\frac{1}{2}$. Ask probing questions that press students to think about these barriers, such as, Is it possible that there is a case between integers? If not, why not? What does it mean for the pattern to shrink past zero? What could that look like? Or does it just stop? Why? During this stage of the exploration, you don't need to convince students that all cases are possible, but generating debate can contribute to later discussions about domain.

- **Are students seeing the relationship between case number and number of squares?** Key to analyzing and representing these functions is defining the variables involved. Some students may perceive the case numbers simply as labels and not as variables that can be used to predict the number of squares in future cases. As students work, listen closely to them for how they are defining the relationships in these patterns. Ask, What are the parts of this pattern that change? Students will likely see that the number of squares changes, particularly in Patterns B, C, and D. But they may struggle with seeing the case number as varying with the number of squares. You might ask, What is the number of squares related to?

- **Are students constructing coordinate graphs beyond the first quadrant?** The construction of the graph constrains what we can see about the pattern and might imply what students believe the domain to be. If you notice students setting up a coordinate plane in only the first quadrant, ask, Are you going to be able to see all the cases you explored in this graph? What might you miss if you include only positive numbers?

- **How are students moving from written descriptions of patterns to algebraic expressions?** Written descriptions of patterns can support students in talking through the relationships that can be abstracted with numbers and symbols. Ask students about the connections between these two representations. If students are struggling to move from verbal descriptions to numbers and symbols, you might ask, How could we record your words using some symbols? For instance, students likely find it more straightforward to abstract numbers and operations than define variables. Ask, What are the variables in this relationship? How might you represent those? What is the relationship between them?

Reflect

What representations of linear functions did you find most helpful?

Task Cards

How do you see the shapes change as the case number increases? Where do you see the new squares? How do you see the shapes change as the case number decreases? What would case −3 look like? What would the 15th case look like? What would case $\frac{1}{2}$ or 0.5 look like?

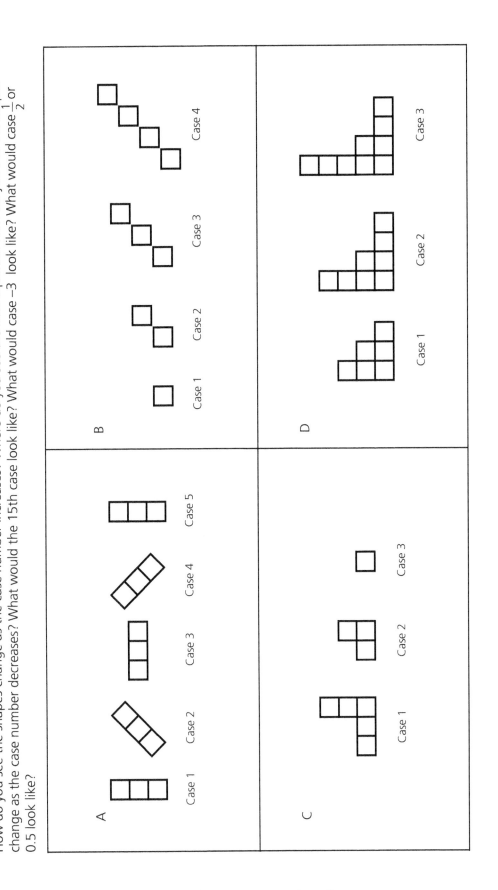

Algebra Representation A

Case 1 Case 2 Case 3 Case 4 Case 5

Make a table using numbers.

Describe the way the pattern is increasing or decreasing.

Make a coordinate graph to illustrate the pattern.

Describe your pattern using an algebraic expression that shows the number of blocks in any case number.

Algebra Representation B

Case 1   Case 2   Case 3   Case 4

Make a table using numbers.

Make a coordinate graph to illustrate the pattern.

Describe the way the pattern is increasing or decreasing.

Describe your pattern using an algebraic expression that shows the number of blocks in any case number.

Algebra Representation C

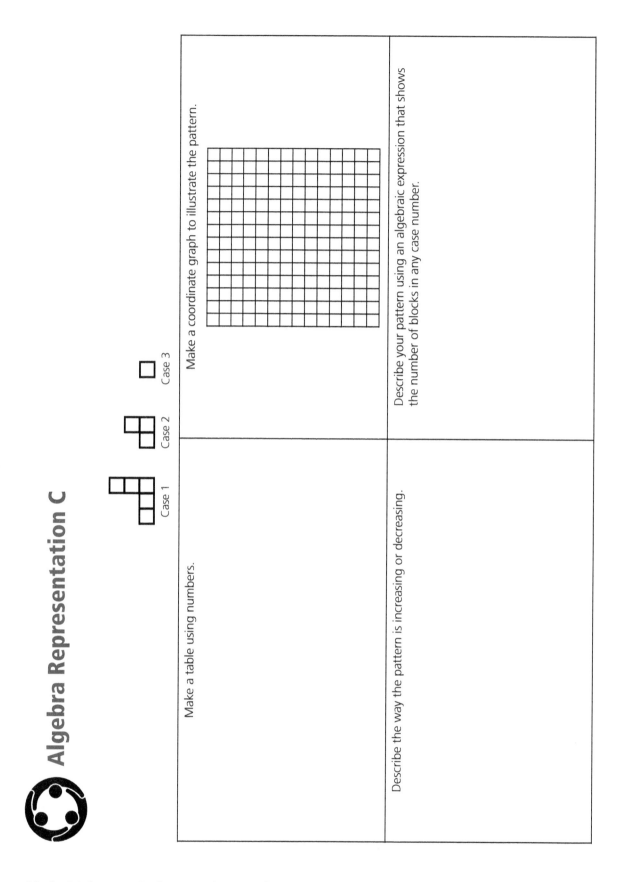

Case 1   Case 2   Case 3

Make a table using numbers.

Describe the way the pattern is increasing or decreasing.

Make a coordinate graph to illustrate the pattern.

Describe your pattern using an algebraic expression that shows the number of blocks in any case number.

Algebra Representation D

Case 1   Case 2   Case 3

Make a coordinate graph to illustrate the pattern.

Describe your pattern using an algebraic expression that shows the number of blocks in any case number.

Make a table using numbers.

Describe the way the pattern is increasing or decreasing.

Make Your Own Function 1

Make a pattern that grows as the case numbers increase.

Draw your pattern. Include at least three representations and label them by case number.	Make a table using numbers.
Make a coordinate graph to illustrate the pattern.	Describe your pattern using an algebraic expression that shows the number of blocks in any case number.

Make Your Own Function 2

Make a pattern that gets smaller as the case numbers increase.

Draw your pattern. Include at least three representations and label them by case number.	Make a table using numbers.
Make a coordinate graph to illustrate the pattern.	Describe your pattern using an algebraic expression that shows the number of blocks in any case number.

Getting Warmer!

Snapshot

Students explore a visual representation of the relationship between Celsius and Fahrenheit, using it to predict temperature conversions not shown and to generalize a linear function.

Connection to CCSS
8.F.4, 8.F.5, 8.F.3, 8.EE.5, 8.F.2

Agenda

Activity	Time	Description/Prompt	Materials
Launch	10 min	Show students the Getting Warmer Function sheet and ask how they see it growing. Color-code student responses on the sheet. Tell students that this image represents the relationship between Celsius and Fahrenheit.	• Getting Warmer Function sheet, to display • Colors
Play	40 min	Partners explore the visual representation of the relationship between Celsius and Fahrenheit to predict cases not shown. Students work to generalize the relationship into an equation to represent the function.	• Getting Warmer Function sheet, per partnership • Colors, grid or dot paper (see appendix), and square tiles or Cuisenaire rods, per partnership
Discuss	20 min	Students share the different images they created for cases 30, 40, 3, 12, –5, and –3. Compare different images for the same case number. Discuss how students made sense of this pattern and the generalizations they devised. Discuss why the pattern was shown with cases in multiples of 5.	

Activity	Time	Description/Prompt	Materials
Extend	60+ min	Partners create a visual representation of the inverse function, in which the case number is degrees Fahrenheit and the squares represent degrees Celsius. Students represent the function with a graph and table and analyze the relationship between these and the original function.	Colors, grid or dot paper (see appendix), and square tiles or Cuisenaire rods, per partnership

To the Teacher

In this activity, we use the linear, but complex, relationship between Celsius and Fahrenheit as a concrete example of a function. We invite students to explore a visual representation of this function and puzzle out ways to extend the cases shown. In this pattern, the case number represents the degrees Celsius, while the number of squares represents the equivalent number of degrees Fahrenheit. One key feature of the way the pile pattern for this function is represented is that only cases in multiples of 5 are shown. Focusing on every fifth case comes from the slope of this graph, $m = \frac{9}{5}$, in which every increase in 5 degrees Celsius yields an increase in 9 degrees Fahrenheit. To show whole numbers of squares, so that the value is countable, the pile pattern shows the cases increasing by 5, while a new row of 9 squares is added. We challenge students to think about how to extend this pattern to higher and lower temperatures, and then to consider how to represent the value of cases between multiples of 5. These in-between cases will support students in thinking about the rate of change per degree Celsius.

We encourage you to make available tools for students to physically model and manipulate this function. The obvious manipulatives are square tiles, which mirror the illustration on the pile pattern. But we'd also recommend Cuisenaire rods as a possible tool. Cuisenaire rods are common in elementary mathematics where they are used to model operations, equivalence, and fractions. Each of the 10 different colored rods in the set represent a whole-number unit length from 1 unit to 10 units. In this activity, students can use rods that are 10 units and 2 units long to represent the constant of 32 degrees and rods of 9 units to represent the increase for each increment of five cases. Cuisenaire rods can support students in segmenting the pattern and thinking about the unit rate of 9 degrees Fahrenheit for every 5 degrees Celsius.

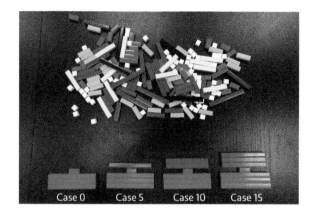

Cuisenaire rods are a useful manipulative for visualizing patterns.

Activity

Launch

Launch by showing students the Getting Warmer Function sheet on the document camera. Ask, What's happening here? What do you notice? How does it grow? Give students a chance to turn and talk to a partner. Take student responses about how they see the function growing and color-code the sheet with what students see.

Tell students that this is a representation of the relationship between Celsius and Fahrenheit, with the case number as the degrees Celsius and the squares as degrees Fahrenheit.

Play

Provide partners with the Getting Warmer Function sheet, colors, grid or dot paper (see appendix), and square tiles or Cuisenaire rods. Partners explore the Celsius-to-Fahrenheit function through the following questions:

- What would case 30 look like? Case 40?
- What would case 3 look like? Case 12?
- What would case −5 look like? Case −3?
- What case (degrees Celsius) would result in 77 squares (degrees Fahrenheit)?
- How can you generalize to the nth case (n degrees C)? That is, how can you predict the number of degrees Fahrenheit for any given number of degrees Celsius?

As students explore this final question, push them to represent the relationship abstractly—to make their equations match the pile patterns they have made.

Discuss

Invite students to share the different images they created for each of the cases 30, 40, 3, 12, −5, and −3. If students have made different representations for a single case, be sure to spend time comparing them and asking what makes sense. Different representations can be accurate, provided that the output (the number of squares) is the same.

As a class, discuss the following questions:

- How did you make sense of this pattern?
- How can we generalize this pattern to predict the number of squares (degrees Fahrenheit) for any case (degrees Celsius)? Compare and contrast different generalizations.
- Why do you think this pattern was shown with cases in multiples of 5 (cases 0, 5, 10, and 15) instead of sequential cases (1, 2, 3, and 4)?
- How did you find the case with 77 squares?

Extend

Provide partners with colors, grid or dot paper (see appendix), and square tiles or Cuisenaire rods. Challenge students to create representations of the inverse function. Ask, If you only had the temperature in degrees Fahrenheit (as with the 77 squares question), how would you predict the temperature in degrees Celsius? Students work to make a pile pattern where the case number represents the degrees Fahrenheit. Partners make a table and graph of their findings and explore the following questions:

- What do you notice about your pile pattern, table, and graph?
- How do these findings relate to the Celsius patterns?

Look-Fors

- **Are students noticing that the cases are not consecutive?** Typically, when we present pile patterns, the cases are consecutive, often starting with case 1. In this pattern, because the rate of change adds a fractional number of degrees with each case, we have shown cases in multiples of 5 so that a whole number of degrees, 9, can be added. For students to begin to grapple with the meaning of this pattern, they first need to notice that the cases are nonconsecutive. This observation may come up in the launch discussion, but even if it does, there may be some students who do not attend to this structure and consider its meaning. Ask students to talk about how the cases are growing and, as they do, press them to use language that describes both how the cases increase and how the number of squares changes. This might sound like, "When you go up 5 cases, you add 9 squares" or "As the number of the case increases by 5, the number of squares goes up by 9." Linking the change in cases to the change in squares will help students think about the rate of change and attend to the case numbers.

- **How are students handling finding cases between multiples of 5?** The fraction involved in this relationship is not easily decomposed to think in increments of a single case. Students may want to estimate the change by saying that each case adds "about 2 degrees," but this is a time for precision. If 2 degrees Fahrenheit were added for each degree Celsius, then the image would look different; the rows on the top would contain 10 squares instead of 9. Press students to be precise by asking, How many degrees (or squares) must be added for each case, so that after 5 cases, we have added 9 squares?

- **How are students thinking about negative cases?** In this pattern, the negative cases still have squares to subtract (for at least the first several cases), but the feature of the pattern that has changed, the number of rows of 9 on the top, is absent in case 0. Students will need to decide which squares to remove and how to organize the results visually. If students are struggling to think about this change, ask, How did the pattern grow? How could you reverse that pattern? What could it look like?

Reflect

Is the relationship between Celsius and Fahrenheit a function? Why or why not?

Getting Warmer Function

Case 0   Case 5   Case 10   Case 15   Case 20

The Functions of Near Squares

Snapshot

Students explore ways to represent and generalize the relationship between the areas of squares and those of near squares, starting with an intriguing pattern in the multiplication table.

Connection to CCSS
8.F.4, 8.F.5, 8.F.2

Agenda

Activity	Time	Description/Prompt	Materials
Launch	10 min	Show students the Multiplication Table Pattern sheet and ask what they notice. Discuss the relationship between the green and yellow shaded cells in the table. Define squares and *near squares*, or rectangles whose dimensions are +1 and −1 of a square.	Multiplication Table Pattern sheet, to display
Explore	45+ min	Partners investigate the patterns in areas of squares and near squares, create a visual representation, and generalize the relationship using symbols. Then partners explore how this relationship changes if, instead of changing the squares side lengths by ±1, the side lengths are changed by ±2, ±3, or any similar value. Students represent this pattern visually and use symbols to generalize the relationships they find.	• Multiplication Table Pattern sheet, per partnership • Square tiles, grid paper (see appendix), and colors, per partnership

Activity	Time	Description/Prompt	Materials
Discuss	20+ min	Discuss the relationships students found, illustrated, and generalized between the areas of squares and the areas of near squares. Compare and connect ways of generalizing. Discuss the different ways that students modified these patterns to explore new relationships. How can the area of the new rectangle be predicted, given the case number? Support students in looking for general relationships across these different patterns.	
Extend	30+ min	Invite students to hunt for and share other patterns or relationships in the multiplication table. Students choose one or more patterns to represent visually and generalize.	• Multiplication Table sheet, per partnership • Square tiles, grid paper (see appendix), and colors, per partnership

To the Teacher

All the way back in the Grade 3 book, we first introduced the notion of near squares. We defined near squares as those that are made by making one side of a square 1 unit longer and the other side 1 unit shorter. An intriguing pattern emerges in the areas of these squares and near squares, which can also be seen in the multiplication table: a near square always has an area 1 square unit less than its partner square. In third grade, students first explored this pattern visually by building rectangles and seeing physically what happened to the area as they changed a square into a near square.

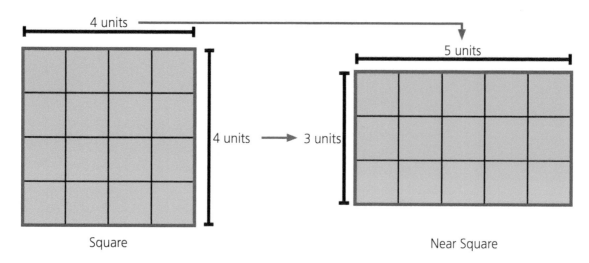

4 units

5 units

4 units → 3 units

Square

Near Square

A 4 × 4 square with an area of 16 square units has a 3 × 5 near square with an area of 15 square units.

Now, for this Grade 8 book, we pose this same pattern as an exploration of functions, so that students can investigate why this pattern exists and how to represent it abstractly. Students now have the tools to begin to formalize the relationships between the side lengths and areas of these two shapes. You'll want to support students as they move toward generalizing the relationship, which might take the form of putting the areas of the squares and near squares on two sides of the equal sign in increasingly abstract ways, such as the following:

$$\text{area of square} - 1 = \text{area of near square}$$

$$\text{side}^2 - 1 = (\text{side} + 1)(\text{side} - 1)$$

$$s^2 - 1 = (s+1)(s-1)$$

As we move further in the investigation, we invite students to consider what happens to the area of the square if, instead of changing the side lengths by ±1, they were to change the side lengths by ±2 or ±3, or even by some larger value. This shifts the pattern out from the diagonal created by the square numbers on the multiplication table farther and farther. Students might similarly explore generalizing these patterns one at a time, so that the generalization for near squares ±2 from squares could be as follows:

$$\text{side}^2 - 4 = (\text{side} + 2)(\text{side} - 2)$$

$$s^2 - 4 = (s+2)(s-2)$$

And the generalization for the near squares ±3 from squares could be as follows:

$$\text{side}^2 - 9 = (\text{side} + 3)(\text{side} - 3)$$
$$s^2 - 9 = (s+3)(s-3)$$

Some students may even see that there is a more general pattern governing all of these relationships; that is, the area can be represented as follows:

$$\text{side}^2 - \text{change}^2 = (\text{side} + \text{change})(\text{side} - \text{change})$$
$$s^2 - c^2 = (s+c)(s-c)$$

Also known as the difference of two squares: $a^2 - b^2 = (a+b)(a-b)$

We have no expectation that students will abstract this larger pattern, but the complexity of the relationships here creates a very high ceiling investigation that students could continue to explore through functions.

Activity

Launch

Launch the activity by showing students the Multiplication Table Pattern sheet on the document camera. Ask, What's going on here? What do you notice? Students may notice connections to the Visualize activity from Big Idea 4 where the number of squares was always a square number, which is the same as the numbers on the diagonal in the multiplication table. They may also notice that there appears to be a relationship between the square numbers in green and the nearby numbers in yellow, what we are going to call the *near squares*.

Tell students that they are going to explore the relationships in these patterns. In these patterns, we're going to consider the length of the side of the square the case number; thus a 5 × 5 square and its near square 4 × 6 are case 5.

Explore

Provide partners with the Multiplication Table Pattern sheet for students to use as they analyze this pattern. Make available square tiles, grid paper (see appendix), and colors. Students investigate the following questions:

- How would you describe the relationship between squares and near squares?

- What does this pattern look like? Create a visual for multiple cases of the squares and the near squares.
- Why does this relationship exist?
- How could you represent the relationship between squares and near squares generally?

Pose the question, What if instead of ±1 to create the near square for each case, we added and subtracted a different value from the side lengths? Explore the following tasks and questions:

- Choose a new variable, or the value used to change the squares, for creating rectangles from a square case. Your pattern could be ±2 or ±3 or anything similar. Generate several cases for your pattern and color-code them on the multiplication table.
- Create a visual representation of your pattern.
- What patterns do you see in the areas of your squares and less-near squares?
- How does the area of your near square relate back to the area of the square number?
- How can you generalize what happens to the area of a square when we change the dimension by adding to one side and subtracting from the other by the same amount?

Discuss

Discuss the initial near-squares relationship:

- How can we describe the relationship between squares and near squares?
- How did you visualize this pattern? (Invite students to share on the document camera the images they created.)
- How could we generalize?

When discussing students' generalizations, highlight ways that use variables or symbols, and make connections between different ways that students developed to communicate the relationship. For instance, students likely developed ways of representing the area of a square; you might color-code the different parts of the generalizations that represent this idea. Making connections between different, but equivalent, forms builds flexibility and students' capacity to interpret new representations.

Discuss the new relationships that students explored:

- What did you find curious about this table and its patterns?
- What variable did you choose for creating new rectangles from squares?
- What relationships did you notice in the rectangles you created?
- How could you predict the area of your rectangles, given the case number?
- How could you generalize the patterns you found?

Look across the patterns that students found using different variables. What do they have in common? This is an opportunity to open up looking for relationships across the patterns that students explored and approaching the general relationship of a difference of two squares.

Extend

Provide students with the Multiplication Table sheet, square tiles, grid paper (see appendix), and colors. Ask, What other patterns or relationships can you find in the multiplication table? Invite students to hunt for and share intriguing patterns through annotating the multiplication table. Encourage students to choose one or more patterns to explore further by investigating the following questions:

- How can you represent those patterns visually?
- How can you generalize the relationships you've found?

Look-Fors

- **How abstract are students' generalizations?** In the teacher note at the opening of this activity, we presented three possible ways students might abstract the relationship between the areas of squares and near squares, moving from a mix of words and symbols toward a more conventional symbolic form. Students are better able to make meaning out of these forms when they have opportunities to see and connect multiple forms of abstraction and visualization. If you notice that students are using only words, you may want to ask if there is a way to use symbols to show the same relationship. However, be sure that students keep all of their representations side by side on their written records, rather than erasing and replacing. Seeing more verbal, visual, and symbolic forms together enables you and students to discuss the connections between them. For instance, you can make connections between the area of a near square written in words with a more symbolic form such as (side − 1) (side + 1), the diagonal rows in the multiplication table for the near squares, and rectangles students have made. This gives the symbols real, concrete meaning, which students at this stage are often at risk of losing if we stop talking about what the symbols represent.

- **Are students looking systematically for patterns in the table?** There are a lot of numbers in the multiplication table, and students may lose track of the patterns they are examining, making it hard for them to find relationships. Highlighting the table to show which cells contain the rectangles of interest can support students in making systematic sense. Students may need to think square by square, asking themselves, If I add and subtract x from the side lengths of this square, what is the new rectangle? Where are those rectangles on this table? You may want to point out that the relationship should form a visible pattern on the table, just as it did with the near squares, and this visible pattern could help students identify mistakes. If students want to explore adding and subtracting a larger number, such as 5 or 6, they may not be able to see much of the pattern on the 12×12 multiplication table. Ask students if they need a larger multiplication table to see this pattern, or whether there is a way to generate the pattern without the table. Students can use grid paper (see appendix) to make their own multiplication table as large as they wish.

Reflect

What different ways of seeing relationships in the multiplication table were most helpful and interesting? Why?

Multiplication Table Pattern

X	1	2	3	4	5	6	7	8	9	10	11	12
1	1	2	3	4	5	6	7	8	9	10	11	12
2	2	4	6	8	10	12	14	16	18	20	22	24
3	3	6	9	12	15	18	21	24	27	30	33	36
4	4	8	12	16	20	24	28	32	36	40	44	48
5	5	10	15	20	25	30	35	40	45	50	55	60
6	6	12	18	24	30	36	42	48	54	60	66	72
7	7	14	21	28	35	42	49	56	63	70	77	84
8	8	16	24	32	40	48	56	64	72	80	88	96
9	9	18	27	36	45	54	63	72	81	90	99	108
10	10	20	30	40	50	60	70	80	90	100	110	120
11	11	22	33	44	55	66	77	88	99	110	121	132
12	12	24	36	48	60	72	84	96	108	120	132	144

Multiplication Table

X	1	2	3	4	5	6	7	8	9	10	11	12
1	1	2	3	4	5	6	7	8	9	10	11	12
2	2	4	6	8	10	12	14	16	18	20	22	24
3	3	6	9	12	15	18	21	24	27	30	33	36
4	4	8	12	16	20	24	28	32	36	40	44	48
5	5	10	15	20	25	30	35	40	45	50	55	60
6	6	12	18	24	30	36	42	48	54	60	66	72
7	7	14	21	28	35	42	49	56	63	70	77	84
8	8	16	24	32	40	48	56	64	72	80	88	96
9	9	18	27	36	45	54	63	72	81	90	99	108
10	10	20	30	40	50	60	70	80	90	100	110	120
11	11	22	33	44	55	66	77	88	99	110	121	132
12	12	24	36	48	60	72	84	96	108	120	132	144

Finding Patterns in the Clouds

As I write this, I am working on a campaign with economist Steve Levitt, one of the coauthors of *Freakonomics,* to bring data analysis more centrally into school mathematics. The need for such a move seems critical. Levitt gathered important information highlighting the fact that our world is now filled with data—every second of every day, the world creates enough data to fill 50 Libraries of Congress, and 90% of the world's data has been created in the last two years (Domo, n.d.; www.freakonomics.com, n.d.). Students leaving school will need to be making sense of "big data," in their lives and in their work. Levitt and his team illustrate the need by considering the job of a car mechanic, which used to be a physical job, but now involves considerable data analysis and computer literacy. In a survey of employers, 40% say they find it difficult to find people who are skilled working with data (Ignatova, 2017). I think of data analysis as quantitative literacy—mathematics in the world—and we are clearly not preparing students well enough in this area. Surveys of recent graduates show that when they reach the workplace, they wish they had been better prepared in data science and data visualization, not algebra or geometry (www.freakonomics.com). In this set of activities, we invite students to develop critical understandings of quantitative literacy.

A lovely accompaniment to data science and analysis is the growing field of *data visualization*—the visual representation of data—with creators suggesting many new and creative ways of representing data that go beyond the traditional bar graphs and pie charts. This big idea is filled with opportunities for students to read and analyze data and to create their own data visualizations.

In our Visualize activity, we share with students graphs from the *New York Times* website "What's Going On in This Graph?" (www.nytimes.com/column/whats-going-on-in-this-graph). We encourage students to read the graphs fully to learn as much as they can from them. They should also be encouraged to take account of the structure of the graphs—the axes, labels, and scales, and the trends that they perceive in the data. We also give students the opportunity to collect their own graphs, looking in particular for intriguing data displays that they can find and bring back to the classroom for discussion with the rest of the class.

In our Play activity, we get playful with students by presenting two graphs, with real data, that are a little off. The first graph has some missing data, so we ask students to construct a story that matches the data and to complete the missing data. Students will develop and present their stories and graphs, and ask questions of one another. They then get to choose the story they found to be most convincing and create a written explanation for the reasons why, considering what the data shows and any connections to the stories students created. The second graph is deliberately misleading. This will give students the opportunity to develop an important critical eye when looking at data representations. They live in a world in which data is often presented to be misleading, and we hope this activity helps them learn to be aware of the need to think critically when looking at data.

In our Investigate activity, students will be invited to create their own data visualization, either from a data set we provide or one they find on their own. This is an opportunity for students to think creatively while also being true to the data. They should think about the ways that different data displays highlight different aspects of data, and give a true and interesting representation.

Jo Boaler

References

Domo. (n.d.). Data never sleeps 6.0. https://www.domo.com/learn/data-never-sleeps-6

Ignatova, M. (2017, December 7). Here are the 20 fastest-growing jobs in the US. *LinkedIn Talent Blog.* https://business.linkedin.com/talent-solutions/blog/trends-and-research/2017/here-are-the-20-fastest-growing-jobs-in-the-us

What's Going On in This Graph?

Snapshot

Students explore complex data displays, building habits of inquiry and interpretation for bivariate data.

Connection to CCSS
8.SP.1, 8.SP.4

Agenda

Activity	Time	Description/Prompt	Materials
Launch	10 min	Show students the Climate Graph (see link in Launch section) or other complex data display. Ask, What do you notice? What is being represented? Give students a chance to turn and talk, then discuss students' observations.	Complex data display, such as the Climate Graph, to display
Explore	30–40 min	Partners use complex data displays and a set of guiding questions to examine what is being represented and the possible meanings of the data. Students mark up their displays to show their interpretations and questions.	• Guiding Questions for Examining Data Displays sheet, per partnership • Copy of the data display shared in the launch, per partnership • Colors, per partnership • Access to other complex data displays
Discuss	15–20 min	Discuss the different data displays that students examined, using the guiding questions as a frame. Compare the different graphical forms and what they enabled the reader to see.	

Activity	Time	Description/Prompt	Materials
Extend	Ongoing	Students collect and bring back to class creative, intriguing data displays that they may encounter in the world. Using the guiding questions, discuss the different displays students find.	Optional: online or print resources with complex data displays

To the Teacher

In this big idea, we explore relationships in bivariate data, or data with linked pairs of numerical observations. These pairs do not need to have a fixed relationship, such as a linear or quadratic relationship. Most of the data in the real world is bivariate data, such as the weight of an animal in relation to its heart rate, or crime frequency in relation to the city population. Relationships exist between these variables, but they are associations that create patterns or trends, rather than predictable outputs for given inputs. Bivariate data like this requires people to interpret the possible meanings in the data, considering what is shown, what is missing, and the meanings of outliers. For instance, in examining bivariate data of crime frequency in relation to city population, we might see that crime increases with population; however, a host of other factors are missing from this association, such as race and policing practices, poverty, and the availability of community supports. These missing factors could help us understand why some smaller communities have much higher apparent crime rates than others. Making meaning out of patterns, interrogating patterns in data, and looking for alternative explanations are all crucial practices in statistics that we hope engage students in during this activity.

We have structured this activity with the intent that you could choose what kinds of bivariate data students interact with. We've done this for two key reasons. First, we want the data to be relevant to your students and their community. We encourage you to look for topics and data sources that speak to important and engaging issues that your students and their families may face. This might include pollution, school funding, crime, access to services, municipal spending, college admissions, or jobs. Second, data changes. To make informed interpretations, we want students to have access to the most current data possible. We launch this activity by recommending a graph related to historical climate change, which indicates that 2018 was the fourth-hottest year on record, a statistic that is likely to be overshadowed by data for 2019 and beyond.

Given that there is value in locating your own data, where can you find intriguing data displays? We have been very excited by a series from the *New York Times* aimed at educators and students called "What's Going On in This Graph?" from which we have taken the title of this activity. In this series, the paper draws on data displays that its staff and others have created for articles in the newspaper, and encourages students to interact with them as sense makers. These are complex displays of data designed to show multiple and thought-provoking relationships. Each of the displays requires careful interpretation of the axes, color-coding, keys, units, graph type, variables, and relationships. For example, in the Climate Graph from this series that we recommend for the launch, readers need to attend to how the *y*-axis is scaled to show the data's relationship to the mean global temperature from 1880 to 1899 and to infer that the color-coding is intended to show intensity of deviation from this mean, both hotter (pink) and colder (blue). Other newspapers, periodicals, and government reports similarly produce dense graphical representations of data in a variety of forms, many of which students may not have seen before when tackling simple bar, line, and pie graphs. For this activity, you can use data displays from the *New York Times* series or any source that you think would be provocative for your students. We recommend that you have on hand at least four different data displays that students can explore.

Activity

Launch

Launch the activity by showing students the Climate Graph (https://www.nytimes.com/interactive/2019/02/06/climate/fourth-hottest-year.html) or another complex graphical representation on the projector. Ask, What do you notice? What is being represented? Give students a chance to turn and talk to a partner. It may take students a few minutes to think about this image. Discuss what students see and how they are making sense of the graph. Invite students to come up and point out features of the graph that they are using to make sense out of what it shows.

Explore

Provide students with the Guiding Questions for Examining Data Displays sheet, a copy of the data display shared in the launch, and colors. Students explore the guiding questions to try to make sense of the graph and what it is communicating.

Provide students with access to other complex data displays. Students use the same set of guiding questions to annotate (or make notes on) multiple data displays and then discuss each as a whole class.

Discuss

Discuss the different graphs that students examined, starting with the data display used in the launch, and talk through the guiding questions:

- What do you notice?
- What is being represented?
- What patterns do you see?
- What does it make you wonder?
- What important data might be missing from this display?
- What other ways could you represent this data?
- What conclusions does this graph/display point you toward (or suggest)?
- What more do you want to know?
- How does this kind of display communicate findings about the data?
- What do you think the author's purpose was in constructing this graph?

Make connections between the various types of data displays that students examined and point out the ways that different kinds of displays offer different opportunities to see and understand data.

Extend

Invite students to find interesting data displays in the world to bring back to the classroom. This could serve as a standing task or one in which you create deliberate space for students to look for data displays through trusted sources online or in print. Make a wall for displaying and discussing these. Use the guiding questions from this activity as a structure for examining graphs that students contribute. These displays can then be an inspiration for the investigation later in this big idea.

Look-Fors

- **Are students attending to the structure of the graph, including axes, scales, and labels?** The details of a graph's structure are often literally marginalized, appearing at the edges of the image, with the data at the center. But the structure of the graph provides crucial information about the variables being compared, the magnitude of differences or trends, and the range of the data being reported. Encourage students to begin by examining the structure so that they can make sense of the data and its relationships. Ask, How is this data organized? What data is being shown? Where does the data start and end? What units are being used?

- **Are students inferring information not shown?** Sometimes data displays rely on the reader bringing outside knowledge to the display to make meaning. For instance, in the Climate Graph, it is useful if students have an understanding of when the mass production of automobiles began or when World War II occurred. In data displays that are overlaid on a map, readers can make sense of the data better if they understand the underlying map, such as knowing where cities or rural areas are located. Where outside knowledge might be helpful in interpreting or posing questions about data, ask students questions to help them access that information, such as, What do we know about that time period? or What do you want to know about the map to help make sense out of the pattern you noticed? Students may not have this information themselves, so create opportunities for them to talk to others in the class who may, or consult online or print resources.

- **Are students posing critical or curious questions about the data?** These data displays should be taken as launching pads for inquiry, and we have deliberately tried to elicit student questions about data. Encourage students to ask questions about the data, both those that are purely curious and those that critique the ways the data are displayed. For instance, students may wonder what's driving a trend in the data and suggest some factors that could be involved. They might also suggest that these other factors are more important than the graph implies, perhaps leading to overly simplistic conclusions. Encourage students to consider the question, What other explanations for the data are possible? Students may also pose questions that move beyond the data itself, such as, What can we do about this trend? Data can be a catalyst to action and advocacy, and we encourage you to foster opportunities for students to act on data, particularly when the data comes from and reflects issues in their own communities.

- **Are students thinking about relationships?** At the heart of examining bivariate data is looking for relationships. Encourage students to think about the relationships that the data display is suggesting, even while they question those relationships. Support students in thinking and talking about relationships by asking, What relationships do you see in this data? What relationships does this data display suggest? What other factors might there be in those relationships?

Reflect

Which data display did you find most thought-provoking? Why? What did the creator of that display do to communicate what you found interesting?

Guiding Questions for Examining Data Displays

- What do you notice?

- What is being represented?

- What patterns do you see?

- What does it make you wonder?

- What important data might be missing from this display?

- What other ways could you represent this data?

- What conclusions does this graph/display point you toward (or suggest)?

- What more do you want to know?

- How does this kind of display communicate findings about the data?

What's the Story Here?

Snapshot

Students play with the stories that graphs tell by examining two types of graphs, one that is incomplete and one that is deceptive.

Connection to CCSS
8.SP.1, 8.SP.4

Agenda

Activity	Time	Description/Prompt	Materials
Launch	5–10 min	Show students the Mystery Scatterplot sheet and ask them what they notice. Be sure that students see that several pieces of information are missing from the graph.	Mystery Scatterplot sheet, to display
Play	20 min	Groups develop a story for the data in the Mystery Scatterplot that explains what the graph shows, any outliers or trends, and the domain of the data. Students complete the missing details in the graph so that it matches their story.	• Mystery Scatterplot sheet, per partnership • Colors, per partnership
Discuss	20 min	Each group presents their story and labeled graph, and students ask questions of one another. Each group then chooses the story they found most convincing and creates a written explanation for why. Reveal what the data really shows, and discuss its story and any connections to the stories students created.	Women in Congress sheet, to display

Activity	Time	Description/Prompt	Materials
Play	15–20 min	Groups examine the Mystery Graph and develop a story and title for the data, which they will share with the class. Students' stories must account for all the features of the graph, including the axes, labels, and units.	Mystery Graph sheet, per partnership
Discuss	15–20 min	Debate the story that the Mystery Graph tells, and focus the discussion on how the deception of the graph distorts the story the data tells.	Mystery Graph sheet, to display
Extend	Ongoing	Students look for and bring back examples of deceptive graphs in the world. Create a display space where students can post and annotate deceptive graphs.	Display space

To the Teacher

In this activity, we play with the notion that data tells a story. In the Visualize activity, we encouraged students to interpret the story that different data displays might be telling. Here, we invite students to create convincing stories of data by sharing a graph that is missing so many labels that it is impossible to tell what the real story is. The data shows that the *x*-axis is *year,* and there is a discernible slow upward trend. Students will need to consider what variables might change in this way with time and describe the variable, label the axes, and provide a title that might explain the pattern. The scatterplot actually shows the number of women in Congress over the last century, as shown in a second, labeled graph that you can share during the first discussion.

In the second half of this activity, we ask students to extend their work telling the story of data, but this time the graph that students explore is deceptive. Deceptive data displays are common in the media, where axes, units, domains, or the context of the data itself can be intentionally distorted to make the story of the data appear to be one thing, when in fact the story may be far less dramatic or more nuanced. We've borrowed techniques for distorting data displays from Darrell Huff's classic book

How to Lie with Statistics, which could be a useful source for extending this work on critiquing graphs even further.

Activity

Launch

Launch the activity by showing students the Mystery Scatterplot sheet on the document camera. Ask students, What do you notice? Give students a chance to turn and talk with a partner. Discuss students' observations, and be sure to point out that several pieces of crucial information are missing from this data display.

Play

Provide groups with the Mystery Scatterplot sheet and colors. Each group develops a story that goes with the data and the missing labels that would complete the graph, including a title. Groups should be prepared to tell the story of the data with the goal of persuading the class that their story best explains the graph. Groups should be sure their story includes the following:

- A title for the graph and an explanation of the variable on the y-axis
- An explanation for the variation in the data, both the trends and any outliers
- A description of the domain of the graph, where the data starts and ends

Discuss

Invite each group in turn to share their graph with labels on the document camera and tell their story of the data. Ask students to listen for convincing evidence that the story makes sense with the graph. Invite students to ask questions of each group about how the story explains the data.

After all groups have shared, ask the class, Which story did you find the most compelling or convincing? Ask each group to come to agreement within their group about which story was most convincing. Each group then constructs a written explanation of the story they selected and why it makes sense with the data.

Then you can reveal what the scatterplot actually shows. Put the Women in Congress graph on the document camera and ask students, What's the story that the data actually shows? What surprises you? Be sure to highlight any connections to the stories students invented.

Play

Provide students with the Mystery Graph sheet. Partners play with the question, What's the story here? Partners interpret the graph and create a story for the data that they are ready to share with the class. Students consider the following:

- What story explains the relationship in this graph?
- How does your story account for all the parts of the graph (axes, labels, units)?
- What title would you give to the graph?

Discuss

Discuss the Mystery Graph using the following questions:

- What's the story of this graph? Encourage debate.
- What title would you give to the graph?
- How does the construction of the graph shift the way we interpret the story?

Focus the discussion on the deception of the graph and how the way it is structured could lead the reader to misinterpret the story it tells.

Extend

In this ongoing extension, invite students to look for and bring back examples of deceptive graphs in the world. Create a space to display anything students find, with labels to show where the deception is and how it changes the way the reader might interpret the story the graph tells.

Look-Fors

- **Are the stories students construct accounting for all the information they have?** While the first graph is deliberately incomplete, there is much information embedded in the graph that students will need to account for to craft a convincing story. Ask students, What does the label "Year" represent in your story? What years are represented here? Why does your data begin when it does? What kind of data would increase in the way this data does? What units will you use for the y-axis, and how does this fit with your story? The data points toward continuing increase. How does your trend account for that pattern?

- **Are students attending to the structure of the graph?** In both graphs, but particularly in the second, students need to pay careful attention to the structure of the graph, rather than the illustration of the data. Ask, How are you making sense of the axes? What does each one mean? When does the data begin and end (that is, what is the domain)? Why might that matter for the story you tell about this graph? Support students in thinking through the meaning of the axis labels, the numbers, and the units used, and how the two axes relate to one another, as they construct a story of the data that makes sense with all the parts of the graph.

Reflect

How can you detect a deceptive graph?

Reference

Huff, D. (1954). *How to lie with statistics*. New York, NY: Norton.

Mystery Scatterplot

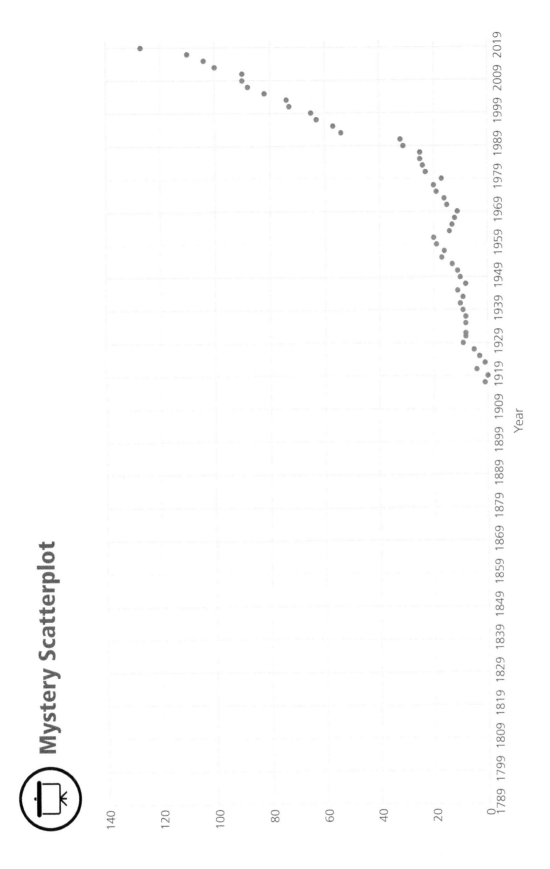

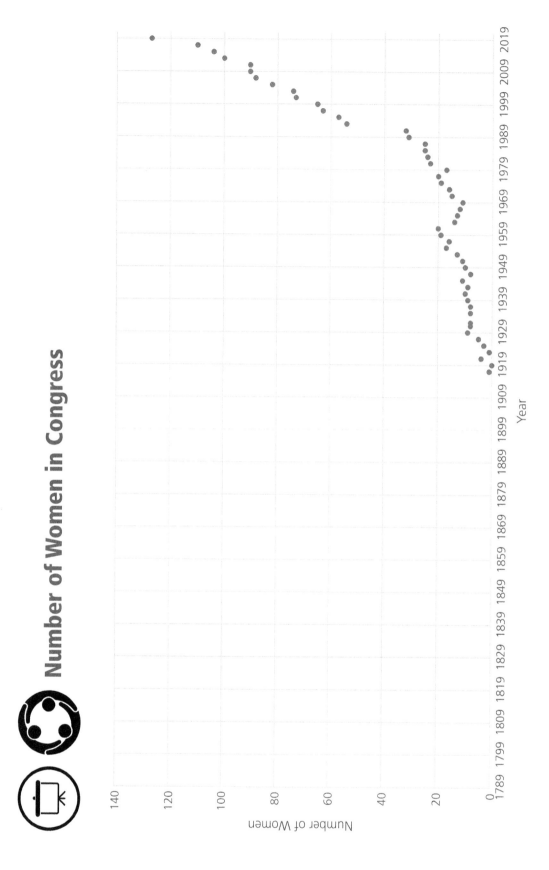

Number of Women in Congress

Number of Women

Year

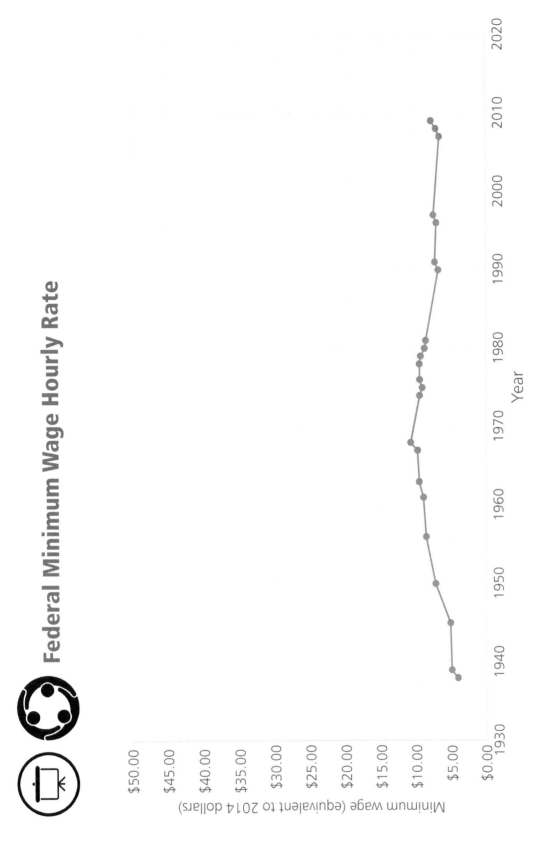

Federal Minimum Wage Hourly Rate

Minimum wage (equivalent to 2014 dollars)

$50.00
$45.00
$40.00
$35.00
$30.00
$25.00
$20.00
$15.00
$10.00
$5.00
$0.00

1930   1940   1950   1960   1970   1980   1990   2000   2010   2020

Year

Creating Data Visualizations

Snapshot

Students investigate real, publicly available data and explore creative ways to display the patterns they find.

Connection to CCSS
8.SP.1, 8.SP.4

Agenda

Activity	Time	Description/Prompt	Materials
Launch	15 min	Show students data visualizations and describe this as an emerging field. Show students the Educational Attainment 2018 Data Set and ask students what it shows. Discuss the variables represented. Ask students how they might display this data, and discuss the possibilities and the need to limit what is displayed.	• Examples of data visualizations, to display (see To the Teacher section) • Educational Attainment 2018 Data Set, to display
Explore	80+ minutes	Groups use either the provided data set or one they find themselves to explore patterns in real data. Groups discuss what relationships might exist in the data and develop plans for how they could display these patterns. Groups use tools to create interesting data displays that highlight the patterns they want readers to notice.	• Educational Attainment 2018 Data Set, for each group • Access to additional data sets (see To the Teacher section) • Make available: grid paper (see appendix), dot paper (see appendix), colors, rulers, examples of creative data displays, Excel, calculators, compasses, and protractors

Activity	Time	Description/Prompt	Materials
Discuss	20+ min	Groups post their displays and do a gallery walk, trying to interpret the displays of others. Discuss what students found most compelling in their own data and the decisions they made about how to display it. Discuss what was challenging about creating data displays and what features made them most effective at communicating patterns or relationships.	
Extend	25+ min	Discuss how students might take action on the patterns of injustice or inequity they have noticed in their data or the data others shared. Make a plan together for what that action might look like, and designate time to carry out the plan.	Varies

To the Teacher

In the launch of this activity, we ask you to share examples of data visualizations or infographics that you think students would find compelling and intriguing, and talk about this new field. Data visualization has emerged as indispensable as both the quantity and complexity of data we collect have exploded. These visualizations make it possible to detect patterns that might otherwise go unnoticed. Unlike the connection between *x* and *y* variables, these patterns are rarely simple. Instead, data involve multiple variables and multiple potential patterns; choosing what data to display and how to display it can draw more attention to some of these patterns than others. In the course of this investigation, you'll want to remind students of the ways that data display choices can distort the story that data tells, which they explored in the Play activity.

Where can you find intriguing data visualizations? Searching for *data visualizations* or *infographics* online may be the most effective way to find a broad menu of current data displays. The *New York Times* series "What's Going On in This Graph?" (www.nytimes.com/column/whats-going-on-in-this-graph), which we explored in the Visualize activity, can serve as another resource, as can the Wikipedia page on data visualizations (https://en.wikipedia.org/wiki/Data_visualization). In addition to online resources, several texts have been published in the last five years that focus on the art of infographics. We particularly like *Understanding the World: The Atlas of Infographics* by Sandra Rendgen (2014), but you may well find others at your local library.

For this investigation, we invite students to explore data sets and how they might create illuminating visualizations of that data. We encourage you to make ample time for this investigation and to open, as much as possible, opportunities for students to find the kinds of data they are interested in exploring and displaying. Perhaps the most powerful source of data about people in the United States is the US Census Bureau, whose website (www.census.gov) offers access to vast volumes of data in spreadsheets and customizable reports. It provides data at the national and state levels, across time, and focused on multiple aspects of people's lives, including education, housing, income, employment, and health. We have edited one report on educational attainment to focus on employment to use in the launch and for students to explore. (You can find the full report in a spreadsheet at www2.census.gov/programs-surveys/demo/tables/educational-attainment/2018/cps-detailed-tables/table-2-1.xlsx.) The data comes from the Current Population Survey's 2018 Annual Social and Economic Supplement, and you can find additional years of this data at the Census Bureau's educational attainment data tables site (www.census.gov/topics/education/educational-attainment/data/tables.2018.html).

In addition to the Census Bureau, other governmental bodies release data to the public on issues ranging from climate and ecosystems to agriculture and manufacturing through their central hub (www.data.gov), which catalogs over 200,000 data sets. Your local community, at the state, county, or municipal level, may also offer data sets to the public that could speak to issues of local importance or compare trends at a smaller grain size.

We encourage you to use these publicly available spreadsheets because they will enable students to explore the data display tools embedded within Excel. Although these tools do not create displays as creative as those you might show students in the launch, they can support students in deciding what kinds of displays reveal the most interesting patterns. Students can use or modify these displays or create their own by hand.

One final note on using real data: We think it is vital that students have access to real data and have opportunities to explore topics of consequence in their lives and communities. These topics might involve social issues, such as school funding inequities, incarceration, crime, food waste, or pollution, each of which raises questions about justice and equity. Further, census data can include or exclude categories that bring inequities involving race, gender, home language, marital status, and citizenship into stark relief. The census data, for example, offers only two gender choices, which do not fully account for the ways that all people identify. We think that using data to unearth and address meaningful issues with your students is critical work, and in preparing for it, you should consider what difficult or triggering conversations may be raised by your students. In the extension, we invite you and your students to consider how to turn what you find into action. Taking action on injustice will both empower your students and shed light on one reason that mathematics is crucial for everyone.

Activity

Launch

Launch the activity by showing some examples of intriguing, surprising, and engaging ways that people have developed for displaying data, using print or online resources. Tell students that this is now its own field: data visualization. Data visualization is becoming an increasingly important field of study because we generate more data now than ever before. Finding new ways to see and interpret this data is critical. These displays help us see patterns and connections that might be otherwise invisible.

Show students the Educational Attainment 2018 Data Set, and tell them that this data comes from the US Census Bureau. You can either share the edited data set we've created or download and display the spreadsheet of the data from the US Census Bureau website (see To the Teacher). Ask, What does this data show? Give students a chance to turn and talk to a partner, and then take some observations about the variables being compared.

Ask, How we might display this data? Give students a chance to turn and talk to a partner, and then take some ideas. Be sure to draw attention to the idea that including all of the data in a single display would be either impossible or overwhelming. To display the data, we would have to decide what parts of it to display and how. If you are sharing the Excel version of the data, you might show students how to use the "Charts" options to explore what different types of displays offer.

Explore

Provide each group with access to the Educational Attainment 2018 Data Set, either in print or electronically, and access to tools to find their own data sets (see To the Teacher for websites). Partners work together to explore the patterns in the data, using the following questions:

- What does this data show?
- What relationships seem most interesting? Which variables might be connected?
- How could we look for relationships that are difficult to see in data tables?

Partners work together to develop a display that communicates something provocative about the relationships in the data they have identified or suspect. Students can use Excel or digital tools, or create displays by hand. Don't rush students to make a display too fast. Encourage students to explore different possibilities for relationships and data displays before making a decision. Students explore the following questions:

- What creative ways of showing the data can you think of?
- What could these displays say about the relationships in the data?

If students are working by hand, provide access to grid and dot paper (see appendix), colors, and rulers. Make available examples of creative data displays, Excel, calculators, compasses, and protractors. If students want to display data on a map, such as heat mapping by state, you may want to provide access to map templates, often available online. Each group works to create an intriguing data display that others could use to learn something interesting about the data.

Discuss

Post all the data displays and hold a gallery walk. As students walk, ask them to consider the following questions:

- What's the story here?
- What does this display enable you to see in the data?
- What questions does this data display raise? What does it make you wonder?

As a class, discuss the following questions:

- What did you find most interesting in your own data?
- How did you decide which parts of your data to highlight?
- How did you decide what data display to construct?
- What displays did you consider making but rejected? Why?
- How did you construct your display? What did you have to think about? What were you trying to communicate? What did you want your readers to see or understand?
- What was hard about creating a data visualization?
- What data displays did you see around the room that were effective at communicating? What about those displays helped you understand the data?

Extend

The patterns students found may spark a sense of urgency about injustice. If you notice conversations about unfairness or inequity bubbling up during students' work time or the class discussion, we encourage you to discuss and plan for possible advocacy. Discuss the following questions:

- What could you do about the patterns you've found?
- What do you think people need to take action on?
- What might that action look like?
- Who has the power to act on these patterns?

Invite students, either collectively or in groups, to make plans for how to advocate for the change they think is needed. This might look like creating presentations to share data, writing letters, starting a petition, meeting with local decision makers, or educating your community. Set aside time for students to carry out their plans.

Look-Fors

- **Are students studying the data tables? Are they selecting key variables to compare?** Data tables, particularly those publicly available on government websites, can be overwhelming. Simply making sense of the data takes time, and we encourage you to support students to take this time. They will need to consider the variables being offered and compared, what patterns might exist, and how interesting the relationships are. For instance, they might notice that states with larger populations also spend more money on education; this may be less interesting than comparing per-pupil funding that takes into account population size. Some variables may be related (such as income, industry of employment, and educational attainment), and others may be unrelated (such as marital status and state). Choosing which variables to display is the first step in thinking about the relationships that might exist. Students may also want to zoom in on particular comparisons by selecting or transforming the data. For instance, students might not want to compare all 50 states, but instead want to compare your state to one nearby, or to collapse data into regions, such as those in the South versus those in the Midwest. Encourage students to find ways to transform the data to investigate relationships.

- **Are students using data visualization as a tool, rather than as just a display?** One of the key features of data visualization as a field is that the data display is not the final product of data analysis; it is a tool for data analysis. We encourage you, if doing so is at all possible, to make available and support students in using spreadsheets so that they can manipulate data and quickly try out different ways of looking at the data. Seeing slices of the data in different types of graphs could highlight patterns that students have not yet seen or enable students to explore hunches about the data. Point out that this is a process of testing ideas and exploring, rather than a step-by-step process of isolating two variables and constructing a graph. Once students have a sense from these trial visualizations of the patterns they want to highlight, they can customize the displays or build their own by hand, to add complexity or clarity.

Reflect

Why are data visualizations needed?

Reference

Rendgen, S. (2014). *Understanding the world: The atlas of infographics.* Cologne, Germany: Tachsen.

Educational Attainment 2018 Data Set

Table 2. Educational Attainment of the Population 25 Years and Over, by Selected Characteristics: 2018

(Numbers in thousands. Civilian noninstitutionalized population.[1])

		Educational attainment								
	Total	None - 8th grade	9th - 11th grade	High school gradu-ate	Some college, no degree	Associ-ate's degree	Bachelor's degree	Master's degree	Profes-sional degree	Doctoral degree
Total	219,830	8,729	13,682	62,685	35,442	22,369	48,235	21,048	3,172	4,468
Labor Force Status										
Employed	135,851	3,510	5,935	34,152	21,121	15,102	34,943	15,318	2,401	3,368
Unemployed	4,941	209	462	1,652	948	434	860	280	37	59
Not in civilian labor force	79,039	5,010	7,285	26,881	13,373	6,832	12,432	5,450	735	1,041
Occupation Total (Employed Civilians Only)	**135,851**	**3,510**	**5,935**	**34,152**	**21,121**	**15,102**	**34,943**	**15,318**	**2,401**	**3,368**
Management, business, and financial occupations	24,827	178	351	3,533	3,256	2,260	9,884	4,576	296	492
Professional and related occupations	34,439	36	145	2,098	2,981	3,716	12,414	8,519	1,883	2,648
Service occupations	20,719	1,211	1,822	7,705	3,817	2,641	2,942	449	66	66
Sales and related occupations	12,341	119	460	3,379	2,426	1,407	3,711	704	55	79
Office and administrative occupations	14,912	76	360	4,581	3,702	2,096	3,384	616	50	46
Farming, forestry, and fishing occupations	892	244	120	287	87	57	77	14	3	3

Mindset Mathematics, Grade 8, copyright © 2020 by Jo Boaler, Jen Munson, Cathy Williams.
Reproduced by permission of John Wiley & Sons, Inc.

	Educational attainment									
	Total	None - 8th grade	9th - 11th grade	High school gradu- ate	Some college, no degree	Associ- ate's degree	Bachelor's degree	Master's degree	Profes- sional degree	Doctoral degree
Construction and extraction occupations	7,165	662	927	3,185	1,090	656	549	78	10	8
Installation, maintenance, and repair occupations	4,331	144	305	1,805	840	750	414	62	13	-
Production occupations	7,664	492	671	3,463	1,395	809	665	152	7	10
Transportation and material moving occupations	8,562	349	775	4,117	1,527	710	904	147	18	16
Industry Total (Employed Civilians Only)	**135,851**	**3,510**	**5,935**	**34,152**	**21,121**	**15,102**	**34,943**	**15,318**	**2,401**	**3,368**
Agricultural, forestry, fishing, and hunting	2,114	321	167	766	266	178	333	67	10	7
Mining	690	22	34	245	123	64	120	70	7	6
Construction	9,649	683	1,043	3,856	1,547	936	1,273	268	2T	23
Manufacturing	14,442	549	802	4,752	2,255	1,498	3,106	1,188	75	216
Wholesale and retail trade	15,989	268	847	5,304	3,196	1,809	3,655	695	65	151
Transportation and utilities	7,649	147	360	2,829	1,635	802	1,486	363	10	17
Information	2,611	5	41	376	399	230	1,111	398	35	15
Financial activities	10,007	46	121	1,704	1,626	1,094	3,815	1,315	142	144
Professional and business services	17,166	462	601	2,837	2,138	1,620	5,724	2,385	744	654

	Educational attainment								
	Total	None - 8th grade	9th - 11th grade	High school gradu- ate	Some college, no degree	Associ- ate's degree	Bachelor's degree	Master's degree	Profes- sional degree	Doctoral degree
Educational and health services	32,435	259	694	4,874	3,937	4,238	8,893	6,690	989	1,862
Leisure and hospitality	9,300	445	716	3,072	1,709	916	1,997	393	28	25
Other services	6,951	281	434	2,232	1,175	865	1,281	570	37	75
Public adminis- tration	6,849	22	77	1,308	1,115	851	2,149	917	237	173

A dash (-) represents zero or rounds to zero.

[1]Plus armed forces living off post or with their families on post.

Details may not sum to totals due to rounding.

Source: US Census Bureau, Current Population Survey, 2018 Social and Economic Supplement, www.census.gov/ data/tables/2018/demo/education-attainment/cps-detailed-tables.html

BIG IDEA 7

Completing the Real Number System

This big idea focuses on irrational numbers, numbers that are literally not a ratio. Ben Orlin (2018), author of *Math with Bad Drawings,* describes these as "wild and exotic" numbers that are "not only unwhole but unholy" (p. 67). Many of these numbers are famous in mathematics. Pi is probably the most famous, and although pi represents the ratio of a circle's circumference to its diameter, that ratio can never be expressed as whole numbers (although people cheat and call it $\frac{22}{7}$, which is close). The decimal version of pi goes on forever—it never ends, and the numbers never repeat. This is why so many schoolchildren find it fun to try to memorize as many digits of pi as possible.

Another famously irrational number is $\sqrt{2}$. In 2010, Shigeru Kondo calculated $\sqrt{2}$ to one trillion decimal places. Orlin shares an amusing story about his time working in England and his shock to realize that the different paper sizes used there (A4, A5, etc.) are half the length of each other, which means that their length and width all relate to each other with the proportion $\sqrt{2}$. This famous little number appears all through our lives, in photography, music, and planetary movement. The number whose square is 2 is an important one, and one we introduce to students in this big idea.

In our activities, we offer students the opportunity to intuitively understand and derive square roots by showing them squares. This is because all square roots have a lovely visual representation—their square. Side lengths of $\sqrt{2}$ will make a square of area 2; side lengths of $\sqrt{3}$ will give us a square of area 3. When whole numbers are made into squares, the result is a square number. For example, a square of area 4 has sides of length $\sqrt{4}$, or 2. It still surprises me when I meet adults who do not know that square numbers are the numbers that can be arranged as a square. The fact that they have gone through their lives not knowing this tells us that much has gone wrong in mathematics education! Square numbers that can be arranged as squares and triangular numbers that can be arranged as triangles are both beautiful aspects of mathematics.

In our Visualize activity, we show students a floating square and ask them how they would find the area. We made the question deliberately challenging to prompt struggle and brain growth. Students should approach the question using their intuition. The square is rotated so that students cannot simply count the side lengths, and they will need to think creatively about ways to solve the problem. The concept of square roots should emerge from this activity and be highlighted by the teacher. Whenever we have a square root, we know we can create a square!

Our Play activity builds from the Visualize activity, again asking students to think of square roots as sides of squares. Instead of the typical request to make squares out of particular side lengths, we give students areas of squares and ask them to derive the side lengths. The squares we give the students do not have whole-number side lengths, so square roots will be important. Some students may not think squares are possible when sides are not parallel to the axes, so we have included this interesting challenge for them.

In our Investigate activity, students use what they have learned about square roots to develop methods for finding the length of the hypotenuse of a right triangle on a grid. We first ask students to use their intuition and come up with their own ideas for finding the hypotenuse. They share these ideas before being told about any particular method. We know from research (Schwartz & Bransford, 1998) that this is the best way to introduce methods to students—after they have encountered a need for them. This activity should help students make an important connection when they see triangles: thinking about the square that can be drawn from the triangle.

Jo Boaler

References

Orlin, B. (2018). *Math with bad drawings*. Philadelphia, PA: Running Press.

Schwartz, D., & Bransford, J. (1998). A time for telling. *Cognition and Instruction*, *16*, 475–522.

Square Sides

Snapshot

Students build a visual understanding of square roots by finding the areas and side lengths of squares positioned in different ways on a grid.

Connection to CCSS
8.NS.1, 8.EE.2

Agenda

Activity	Time	Description/Prompt	Materials
Launch	10 min	Show students the Floating Square sheet and ask how they would find the area of the square. Take student ideas, which likely involve multiplying the side lengths. Ask how they could find the side lengths with precision. Show students the Gridded Square, and ask how they would find the area of this square using the grid.	• Floating Square sheet, to display • Gridded Square sheet, to display
Explore	30+ min	Partners work to find the areas and side lengths of squares on a grid, organizing their findings in a table to look for patterns. When they think they have found a pattern, they make a set of squares to swap with another group to find the areas and side lengths.	• Square Set sheet, per partnership • Grid paper (see appendix) and ruler, per partnership • Colors, per partnership
Discuss	20+ min	Discuss the strategies students used for finding the areas and side lengths of the squares. Make a table on a chart with the areas and side lengths of the squares and discuss the connection between them. Name the relationship as *square roots* and add this term to your chart.	Chart and markers

To the Teacher

This activity is designed to give students a visual understanding of square roots. Square roots are often defined as irrational numbers, and although this classification is important, it is more useful to see them as the side lengths of a square with a given area. That is, $\sqrt{5}$ is the side length of the square that has an area of 5 square units.

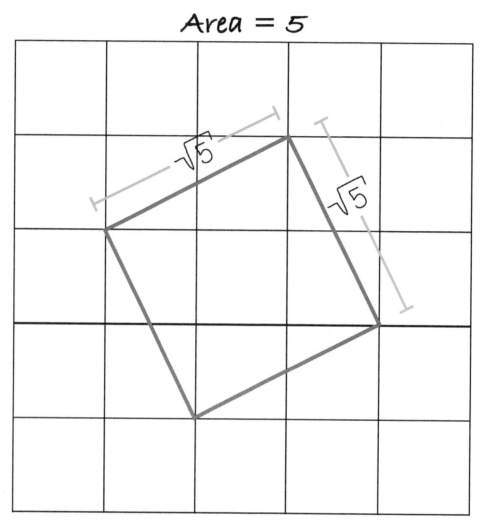

The square has side lengths of $\sqrt{5}$ and an area of 5 square units.

Students may bring with them some ideas about square roots, and we encourage you to build on what students know. However, students may only know the term without knowing what it means or represents. In that case, you'll want to focus attention on the squares themselves and how to think about their areas and side lengths. Use this lesson to motivate defining square roots based on the relationship between the areas and side lengths of squares. Focusing on this relationship will help students in Big Idea 8, where we apply the understanding of square roots to make sense of the Pythagorean theorem.

Activity

Launch

Launch the activity by showing students the Floating Square sheet on the document camera. Ask, How would you find the area of this square? Give students a chance to turn and talk to a partner, and then collect student responses. Students are likely to say that they would find the side lengths and multiply. Pose the question, How would you find those side lengths with precision?

On the document camera, show them the Gridded Square sheet, which shows the same square on a grid. Ask, Considering your methods, how would you use the grid to find the area of this square? Give students a moment to think about the challenges this presents, then send them off to work on the task.

Explore

Provide partners with the Square Set sheet and colors. Partners explore the following questions:

- What is the area of each square? What are the side lengths?
- What is the relationship between the area and the side lengths? Organize your findings in a table.
- For which squares is it challenging to find the area or the lengths of the side? Why?

When partners think they have found a pattern, provide them with grid paper (see appendix) and a ruler. Ask them to create their own set of squares that they could give to another pair of partners to solve. Partners consider the following questions as they make their square set:

- How do you know that the shapes you've created are squares?
- What are the side lengths and areas of your squares? Solve your own tasks to make sure they work.

Students swap with another group and see whether they can find the areas and side lengths of the other group's squares using the patterns they've found.

Discuss

As a class, discuss the following questions:

- What surprised you?
- What were the different strategies that you tried for finding the areas and side lengths? Which worked, and why? Which didn't work, and why?
- Did your strategies work for all the squares? Or did you have to modify your strategies for different squares? Why?
- What are the areas and side lengths of these squares? (Make a class table of values on a chart showing the areas and side lengths.)
- What is the relationship between the area and the side length of a square? (Use student responses to name *square roots* as the side length of a square with a given area. Be sure to add a definition and example to your class chart of the data.)
- When you were making squares, how did you know that the shapes you made were squares?

Look-Fors

- **Are students finding the areas of the squares?** To find the areas of squares rotated on the grid, students will need to consider the relationships among the partial square units. Being precise about the area will involve some form of decomposing of the figure. Students may see the interior of the square as a series of right triangles, where the hypotenuse is the square's side. These triangles can be recomposed into rectangles, making finding the area a straightforward matter. Another way to think about the area would be to draw a larger rectangle—one whose area is easy to find—around the square and then subtract the triangles formed by the extra area. This would again involve thinking about the area of the partial squares and noticing that there are complementary parts that could be joined together to make whole rectangles or whole-unit squares. Although we spent time on this very idea in sixth grade, we find that decomposing shapes on a grid and looking for structure in area can be a challenging project for students throughout middle school. We encourage you not to shortcut students' struggle with developing strategies, as all of these ideas will come back in Big Idea 8.
- **Are students thinking about the side lengths with precision?** If you notice students using language of approximation, such as "about 2 units," remind

them that finding a way to name the side lengths precisely is at the heart of the work they are doing. You might ask, How do you know? Why does that make sense? If students seem to be relying on measurement, ask, How could you use the relationship between area and side length to be more precise?

- **How are students talking about or naming the side lengths?** Students may not arrive at square roots independently, particularly if they have not had previous exposure to this idea. Don't expect students to invent our conventional terms or symbols for square roots. However, you'll want to listen for ways of talking about the side lengths that are conceptually aligned with the idea of square roots and to support students in recording and discussing these lengths. For instance, you might hear a group frustrated because they cannot figure out what number multiplies by itself to get 5. You might then encourage students to write this down in their table using their own words, such as "the number that multiplies by itself to get 5, which is a little more than 2." In the discussion, return to this idea and name for students what we call this value, the "square root of 5" or $\sqrt{5}$.

Reflect

What is a square root?

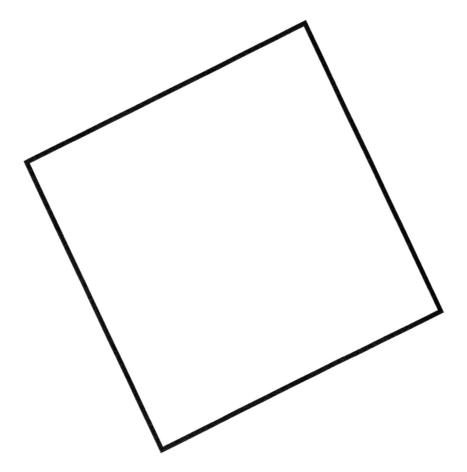

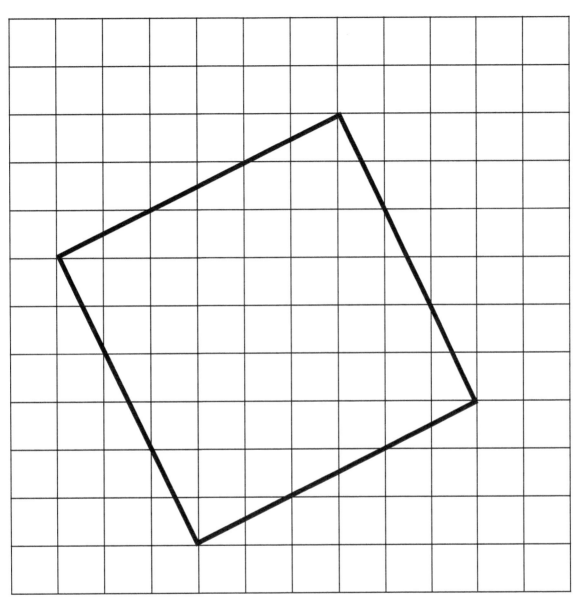

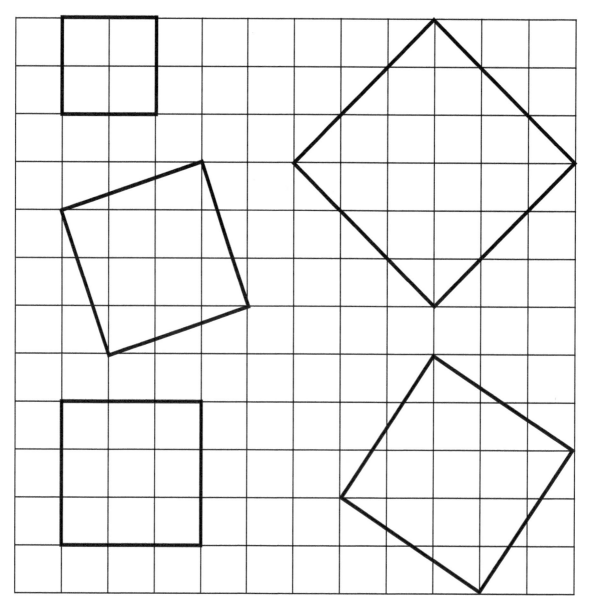

Between 4 × 4 and 5 × 5

Snapshot

Students play with creating squares with irrational side lengths, building on their understanding of square roots as the side lengths of squares with a given area.

Connection to CCSS
8.F.3, 8.NS.1, 8.NS.2, 8.EE.2

Agenda

Activity	Time	Description/Prompt	Materials
Launch	5 min	Remind students of the work they did in the Visualize activity and the definition of square roots they crafted. Show students the 4 × 4 and 5 × 5 Squares sheet and tell them that the side lengths are consecutive whole numbers. Ask, How can you use the grid to make squares with side lengths between 4 and 5 units?	4 × 4 and 5 × 5 Squares sheet, to display
Play	30+ min	Partners play with creating a series of squares where the side lengths are between 4 and 5 units. Students use what they know about square roots to name the lengths of the sides of their squares.	Grid or dot paper (see appendix), rulers, scissors, and colors, per partnership
Discuss	30 min	Partners share the squares they made and their evidence for the side lengths of each one. Create a number line space to post squares in order of side length and discuss as a class how to compare the side lengths of any two squares. Order the squares by side length. Discuss whether the class has found all of the possible squares that can be made on the grid with side lengths between 4 and 5 units. Name square roots that are not whole numbers *irrational numbers*.	Number line with 4 at one end and 5 at the other, with room to post students' squares

Activity	Time	Description/Prompt	Materials
Extend	20–30 min	Partners pick any two consecutive whole numbers and try to create squares with side lengths between them. Students explore whether they can find all such squares.	Grid or dot paper (see appendix), ruler, and colors, per partnership

To the Teacher

The focus of this big idea is exploring the real number system, and in this activity, we are again using geometry to help students attach meaning to numbers that are often difficult to grasp—irrational numbers. Squares give students the opportunity to compare the values of square roots by connecting them to the areas of the squares those side lengths create. That is, $\sqrt{17}$ is less than the $\sqrt{19}$ because the area of the square with side lengths $\sqrt{17}$ is 17 units, a smaller square than that created by one with side lengths of $\sqrt{19}$ units.

During this activity, we invite students to consider whether they can find all of the squares with side lengths between two consecutive integers. This is an interesting question to debate. Although there are infinite squares with side lengths between any two integers, when you consider all potential values for the side lengths, the constraints of this task limit how many of these students can draw. To emphasize square roots and precision, we have included the constraint that students must use the intersection points of the grid (or dots on dot paper) as vertices for their squares. This means that an infinite number of rational side lengths cannot be constructed (for example, 4.1 units, 4.13 units, 4.156 units).

The 4 × 4 square has an area of 16 square units, and the 5 × 5 square has an area of 25 squares units. Students can explore whether they can find ways to construct squares with areas of 17, 18, . . . 23, and 24 square units. When discussing whether they have, or could, find all of the squares that meet the criteria of the task, be sure to draw attention to the ways these constraints take the infinite space between two integers and reduce the number of solutions that are possible.

Activity

Launch

Launch the activity by reminding students of the work they did to find the side lengths of squares in the Visualize activity, and remind them of the definition of *square root* that they developed together. Show students the 4 × 4 and 5 × 5 Squares sheet on the document camera. Point out to students that one of the squares has side lengths of 4 units, and the other has side lengths of 5 units, two consecutive whole numbers. Pose the day's question: How can you use the grid to make squares with side lengths between these integer values?

Play

Provide partners with grid or dot paper (see appendix), rulers, scissors, and colors. Partners play with the following questions:

- If the vertices must be located at intersection points on the grid, what squares can you draw with a side length between 4 and 5?
- How can you be certain that the shapes you have drawn are squares?
- What are the side lengths of your squares? How do you know? Annotate your squares with your evidence.
- How do you know that your square has a side length greater than 4 units and less than 5 units?

Ask students to record each square they make on a separate portion of grid paper so that it can be displayed separately during the discussion. You may want to provide students with half sheets of grid paper for these squares.

Discuss

Invite students to share on the document camera some of the squares they made. Ask each sharing group the following questions:

- What is the length of the side of your square?
- How do you know?
- How can you prove that it is greater than 4 and less than 5?

Create a space on a wall or board for a number line labeled at one end with 4 and the other end with 5. As a class, try to put students' squares in order from side lengths closer to 4 to those closer to 5. Ask the following questions:

- How can we put these squares in order from the shortest side length to the longest?
- What evidence could help us order them?
- How do we know when one side length is longer than another?

In this discussion, be sure to use the area of the square as evidence and continue to support students in reasoning about the length of the sides by thinking about the area of the square they make. After you have ordered the squares, ask, Have we found all the squares with side lengths between 4 and 5? Why or why not?

Name for students that these numbers—square roots that are not whole numbers—are called *irrational numbers*. Tell students that using the square root symbol is the most precise way of naming these irrational numbers.

Extend

Provide students with grid or dot paper (see appendix), ruler, and colors. Invite students to pick two other consecutive whole numbers and try to find a square with a side length between them.

- What methods can you find for doing this?
- Can you find all of the squares with side lengths between your two whole numbers? Why or why not?

Look-Fors

- **Are students drawing on the strategies for finding the areas of squares that they developed in the Visualize activity?** Students will need to use strategic ways to decompose the squares they draw to reason about their areas. We supported students in developing these types of strategies in the Visualize activity, but they may experience struggle as they apply those strategies to this task. Make connections between the ways that students found the areas of the squares in the previous activity and the goal of drawing squares with sides between 4 and 5 units. Ask, How did you find the areas of squares in the Visualize activity? How could those strategies help you with these squares?

- **Are students attending to the constraints of the task?** There are several constraints in this task, and juggling them all can be challenging. Students will likely focus on finding squares with side lengths between 4 and 5 units. However, they must draw *squares,* and those squares must have their vertices at intersection points on the graph. These two constraints are related, because if students do not use the grid, they would find it impossible using the tools they have now to prove that they had drawn a square. With the square located on intersection points, the grid defines the measurements, and any imperfections in the drawing can be disregarded. Ask students how they know they have drawn a square, rather than just a quadrilateral. Press students to use the grid to justify their drawings.

- **How are students reasoning about the relative size of square roots?** This is one case where we discourage the use of rulers as a tool for comparison. Instead, the goal is for students to reason about the size of the squares, particularly their areas, to make sense of the relative lengths of their sides. The areas of the squares have the benefit of being countable and justifiable with precision; by contrast, measurement is necessarily an estimate. Students may wonder if the square root of a larger number is always itself larger. That is, do square roots get larger as the base increases? This is a worthy question to explore, and you may encourage students to think about cases that feel more familiar, such as those with whole-number square roots. For instance, is $\sqrt{16}$ greater than $\sqrt{9}$? Is $\sqrt{9}$ greater than $\sqrt{4}$? Why? What might explain these patterns? Do they apply to numbers like $\sqrt{17}$ and $\sqrt{18}$?

Reflect

How could you estimate the value of a square root, such as $\sqrt{10}$?

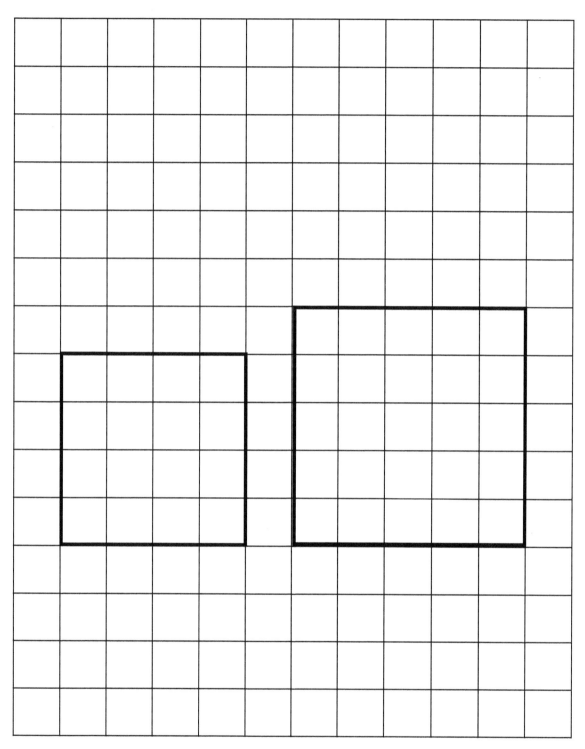

The Hypotenuse Hypothesis

Snapshot

Students use what they have learned about the meaning of square root to develop methods for finding the length of the hypotenuse of a right triangle on a grid.

Connection to CCSS
8.F.3, 8.NS.1, 8.NS.2, 8.EE.2

Agenda

Activity	Time	Description/Prompt	Materials
Launch	5–10 min	Remind students of the work they have done with square roots and tell students that these numbers are precise, not approximations. Show students the Right Triangle sheet and ask, How could we find the precise length of the hypotenuse?	Right Triangle sheet, to display
Explore	40+ min	Partners use the Right Triangle Set to develop methods for finding the length of the hypotenuse. Students then test and refine their methods on triangles they construct themselves.	• Right Triangle Set sheet, per partnership • Grid paper (see appendix), ruler, and colors, per partnership
Discuss	20 min	Discuss and compare the different methods students developed for finding the precise length of the hypotenuse. Discuss how these methods connect back to the area of squares.	

To the Teacher

In this activity, we extend students' thinking about square roots beyond squares by asking students to consider how they might find the length of the hypotenuse of a right triangle. Some right triangles are a quarter of a square, which offers an opportunity for students to connect their previous work to this activity.

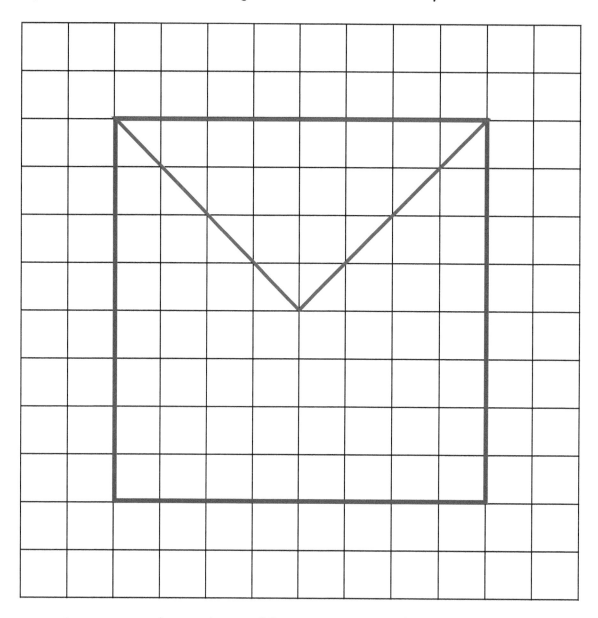

A square can be made up of four congruent right triangles where
the hypotenuse of each triangle is a side of the square.

But all hypotenuses—indeed, any line segment—can be thought of as the side of a square. The triangle as a polygon is not mathematically important for finding the length of its hypotenuse if students reimagine it as the side of a square.

However, we have selected right triangles to investigate here to plant the seed for discovering Pythagoras in Big Idea 8. Do not make the leap to telling students about Pythagoras, and be sure to put the brakes on any student who wants to pull out this formula. Instead, emphasize the need to reason through these lengths and to offer proof that everyone can see and understand.

Activity

Launch

Launch the activity by reminding students of all the work they have done with square roots in the Visualize and Play activities. Point out that these numbers are precise—they are the exact value of the side length, not an approximation. Tell students that when we measure with a ruler, we are always getting an approximation, and sometimes that is all we need. But in the work they will be doing today, we'd like to be precise.

Show students the Right Triangle sheet on the document camera. Ask, How can we find the precise length of the hypotenuse? Give students a chance to turn and talk to a partner to generate some thinking about this task. Encourage students to brainstorm with their partner.

Explore

Provide partners the Right Triangle Set sheet and colors. Partners explore the following questions:

- What is the precise length of the hypotenuse of each triangle?
- What methods can you develop for finding that length?

When partners feel confident in the method(s) they have developed for finding the length of the hypotenuse, invite students to design their own right triangles to test their methods. Provide students with grid paper (see appendix) and rulers. Students investigate the following questions:

- Do your methods always work? Why or why not?
- What modifications can you make so that you can always find the length of the hypotenuse of a right triangle?

Discuss

As a class, discuss the following questions:

- How can you find the precise length of the hypotenuse of a right triangle?
- What different methods did you develop? Which seem to work best? Why?
- What surprised you?
- How did your methods connect back to finding the side lengths of squares?
- What do you wonder now?

Look-Fors

- **Are students thinking beyond the triangles and making connections to squares?** In previous activities, the shape of the square held critical meaning in determining the length of its sides. However, the triangle here doesn't hold the same meaning. That is, there are no "triangle roots." Irrational lengths are still expressed in relationship to the area of the square they might create, even if they are not actually part of that square. Students may begin to think outside the triangle and consider the square whose side is the hypotenuse most readily when they work with isosceles right triangles, which can be seen as one quarter of a larger square with the hypotenuse as one side of the square. Look for students sketching larger squares as signs that they are thinking in this way. With other scalene right triangles, you may need to ask questions to support these connections, such as, How can you use what you know about finding the length of the sides of a square to help you find the length of the hypotenuse? or How could you use what you did with this isosceles right triangle to help find the length of the hypotenuse of a scalene right triangle?

- **Are students using area and square roots to be precise?** There are moments in mathematics for estimates and approximations, which have not gotten enough valued attention in teaching. This big idea, however, is a moment for precision. When we use a grid, we can do something that would be otherwise impossible: draw the length of an irrational number. Consequently, we can do the reverse, which is to find the precise length of an angled line that previously we would have only been able to estimate. The key here is for students to rely again on the conceptual relationship between the area of a square and square roots to be precise. If you notice students arriving at approximations, tell them that this is one answer, but that we'd also like a precise answer. The approximation has value; it helps students understand the relative length of a number like $\sqrt{10}$, and it can serve as a check of reasonableness (that is, Is it reasonable that $\sqrt{10}$ is approximately 3?). So, rather than asking students to stop measuring or estimating, ask them to then find the precise length.

Reflect

How could you find the length of any line segment on a grid?

 **Right Triangle**

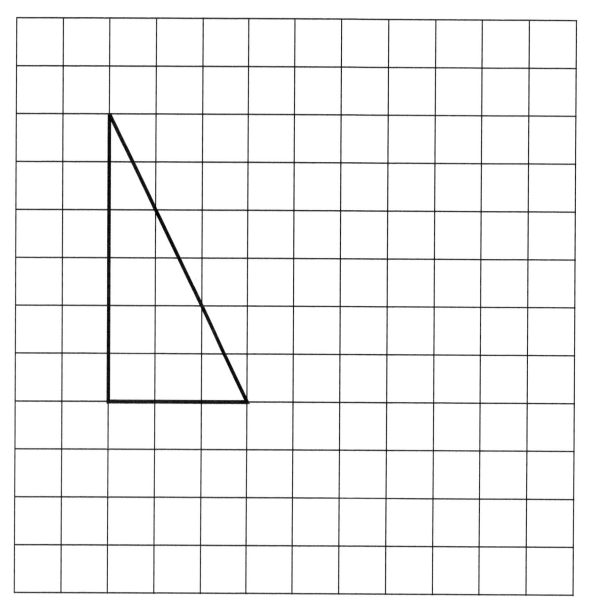

Right Triangle Set

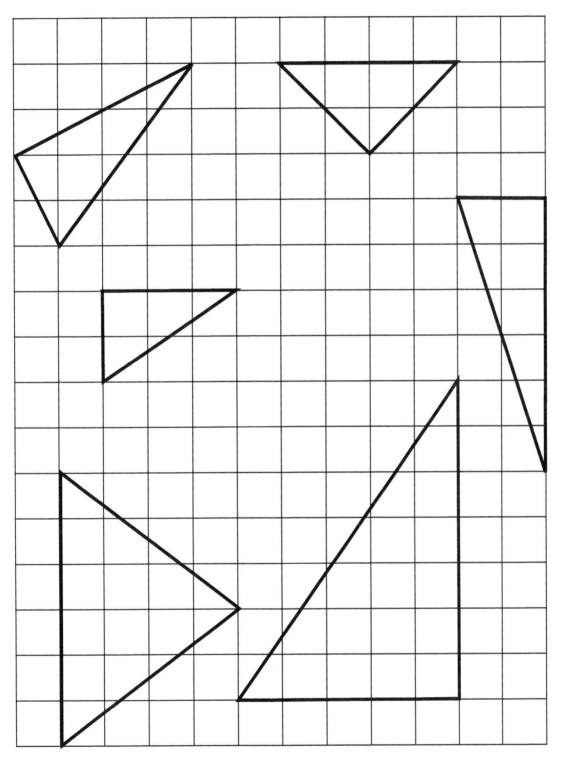

Discovering Pythagoras

When I was taught math in England, as a child, I was taught the Pythagorean formula to use to find the hypotenuse of any right-angled triangle. It was efficient, and I could use it, but it was not enchanting in any way. Having learned mathematics as a set of methods, as most students do, I have always wanted more for students, especially as I have myself been introduced to the beauty of mathematics and the important connections that can be made between ideas. In this big idea, we introduce students to the Pythagorean formula and the Pythagorean triplets in a different way—encouraging them to discover relationships and of course to see them visually.

Harvard educator Eleanor Duckworth once wrote a lovely paper that later became a book called "The Having of Wonderful Ideas." She starts the paper with a description of some interviews she had been conducting with seven-year old children:

> I had cut 10 cellophane drinking straws into different lengths and asked the children to put them in order, from smallest to biggest. The first two 7-year-olds did it with no difficulty and little interest. Then came Kevin. Before I said a word about the straws, he picked them up and said to me, "I know what I'm going to do," and proceeded, on his own, to order them by length. He didn't mean, "I know what you're going to ask me to do." He meant, "I have a wonderful idea about what to do with these straws. You'll be surprised by my wonderful idea." It wasn't easy for him. He needed a good deal of trial and error as he set about developing his system. But he was so pleased with himself when he accomplished his self-set task that when I decided to offer them to him to keep (10 whole drinking straws!), he glowed with joy, showed them to one or two select friends, and stored them away with other treasures in a shoe box. (1972, p. 1)

In her essay, Duckworth (1972) goes on to argue that allowing students to have ideas about mathematical phenomena is the "essence of intellectual development" (p. 1). We often rob students of this opportunity by telling them about relationships they could discover on their own; we present them to students as facts and tell them to memorize them. It is no wonder that students often think they have no opportunities to think for themselves or use their own agency in math class and that they do not develop curiosity about mathematical ideas. Pythagorean relationships are a perfect topic with which to invite students to discover properties of triangles and squares, which is what the activities in this big idea are all about. We hope students will be enchanted to discover these relationships and learn that they map onto our world in interesting ways.

In our Visualize activity, we offer students a visual proof of the Pythagorean relationships ($a^2 + b^2 = c^2$) and ask students whether they can work out what is going on. Some students will know the Pythagorean "formula," but may not have had the opportunity to see it visually and to experiment with it. Students can be encouraged to cut out the squares to look into them further and to explore their relationship, or use another method. In this activity, students will again encounter triangles that do not have integer side lengths, which we connect back to in the next activity.

In our Play activity, students meet a lovely number pattern, called the Pythagorean triple. These are examples of the relationship ($a^2 + b^2 = c^2$) where whole numbers satisfy the pattern. We show students the 3-4-5 right triangle and ask them whether they can find others. Students can use tools, such as square tiles and snap cubes, to search for right triangles that can be made with whole numbers. Pythagorean triples have fascinated mathematicians for centuries; they have studied where these triples occur and the patterns in their occurrence. There is a Wikipedia page devoted to them, which includes interesting representations of the patterns in their occurrence (https://en.wikipedia.org/wiki/Pythagorean_triple). Big Idea 6 talked about interesting data visualizations, and I would count these among them.

In our Investigate activity, we invite students (and their teachers) to engage in a task they have probably never done before! We ask that students fold a 4×4 grid and work to make a number line that shows the positions of the square roots of 1 through 16. In doing so, students will be creating visual proofs of the different numbers, which is a challenging and very cool task.

Jo Boaler

Reference

Duckworth, E. (1972, July). The having of wonderful ideas. http://westoninnovations .pbworks.com/f/The+Having+of+Wonderful+Ideas.pdf

Unpacking Pythagoras

Snapshot

Students unpack the relationship between the side lengths of a right triangle and the squares that can be made by those sides, ultimately naming this as the Pythagorean theorem.

Connection to CCSS
8.G.6, 8.NS.1

Agenda

Activity	Time	Description/Prompt	Materials
Launch	5–10 min	Show students the Squared Right Triangle sheet and ask them what the image is showing. Be sure that students see both the right triangle and the square formed by each side length.	Squared Right Triangle sheet, to display
Explore	30–40 min	Using the squared right triangle as an example, partners explore the areas of the squares, the side lengths of the right triangle, and the relationship between them. Partners then test their conjectures by making their own squared right triangles.	• Squared Right Triangle sheet, per partnership • Dot or grid paper (see appendix), ruler, scissors, and protractor, per partnership
Discuss	20 min	Construct a class data table to organize students' findings about the areas of the squares and the side lengths of the right triangles. Discuss the relationships students found, and test their conjectures with the different right triangles students created. Come to agreement about the relationship and name this as the *Pythagorean theorem*.	Chart paper and markers

To the Teacher

This activity draws heavily on the work students did in Big Idea 7, "Completing the Real Number System." In those activities, we focused on building a geometric understanding of square roots so that students could see these numbers as lengths and compare them. Here, students can build on that idea to explore the relationship among the side lengths of a right triangle and the squares made by the three sides.

Many students may already be able to recite the formula of the Pythagorean theorem, but this does not mean they understand what it represents visually or how to use those relationships meaningfully. If you notice that students want to invoke the formula, ask them to hold back until they can use the images to explain its meaning, which is the goal we hope that students will meet by the end of the activity.

Activity

Launch

Launch the activity by showing students the Squared Right Triangle sheet on the document camera. Ask, What do you notice? What is this image showing? Give students a chance to turn and talk to a partner about what they see. Then take some student observations. Be sure that students notice that the triangle is a right triangle and that there are squares shown whose side lengths are also the lengths of each of the right triangle's sides.

Explore

Provide partners with the Squared Right Triangle sheet, dot or grid paper (see appendix), ruler, scissors, and protractor. Partners use the sample triangle with squares to explore the questions and develop conjectures:

- What are the areas of the squares?
- What are the side lengths of the triangles?
- What is the relationship between the sides and the squares they make?

Once students have developed some ideas using the Squared Right Triangle sheet, partners can test their conjecture(s) about the relationships they found by constructing their own right triangles with squared sides.

Discuss

As a class, discuss the following questions:

- How can we construct a class data table of the triangles and squares you explored? (Determine a way to organize side lengths and square areas for several of the triangles that students constructed, including the one on the Squared Right Triangle sheet.)
- What were the side lengths and areas of the side squares that you found?
- What relationships did you find among the side lengths and the side squares of right triangles? (Use the triangles in the data table to test students' conjectures. Use this discussion to come to agreement about the relationship.)

Name the relationship between the side lengths and the squares they make as represented in the *Pythagorean theorem*, which says that the sum of the squares of the legs is equal to the square of the hypotenuse. Tell students that we often write this as $a^2 + b^2 = c^2$ where a and b are the lengths of the legs and c is the length of the hypotenuse. Record these on the class chart with students' data.

Look-Fors

- **Are any students invoking the Pythagorean theorem without explanation or meaning?** You may hear some students using the name "Pythagorean theorem" or saying "$a^2 + b^2 = c^2$," but when you ask what this means, these students may not yet be able to explain how those terms connect with the image in the Squared Right Triangle sheet. You can ask, What does that mean? Where in this image do you see that formula? Can you connect the parts of that formula to this image? If students struggle, ask them to hold off using terms they cannot explain and instead to focus on making meaning of the image. Press them by asking, What patterns do you see in this image? How could you look for patterns in the squares and side lengths?
- **Are students organizing their findings to look for patterns?** The relationship between the squares made by the sides of a right triangle is not immediately or visually apparent. To explore and make connections, students will need ways of organizing their data. Students might use a table, a color-coded diagram, or an organized list to explore possible relationships. Some methods, such as recording several disconnected calculations, may obscure the very relationships students are looking for. Ask, How could you organize these

findings to look for relationships? What ideas could you test? How could you record your data to make it easier to test your ideas and see connections?

- **Are any students able to explain the meaning of the Pythagorean theorem before the discussion?** You may find that some students are able to explain the meaning of the Pythagorean theorem using the sample triangle. If students can make connections between different parts of the formula and the diagram and describe the relationship between the areas of the side squares of a right triangle, then it is time for those students to put this relationship to the test. Just because this relationship appears to hold up in this diagram does not mean it is *always* true. Invite students to create extreme right triangles to see whether they can find a counterexample. Students might want to test non-right triangles, too, to see the limits of this relationship. Encourage them to bring these findings into the discussion once others have had the opportunity to develop their own thinking.

Reflect

What might the relationship between the side lengths of a right triangle and the squares of its sides be useful for?

Squared Right Triangle

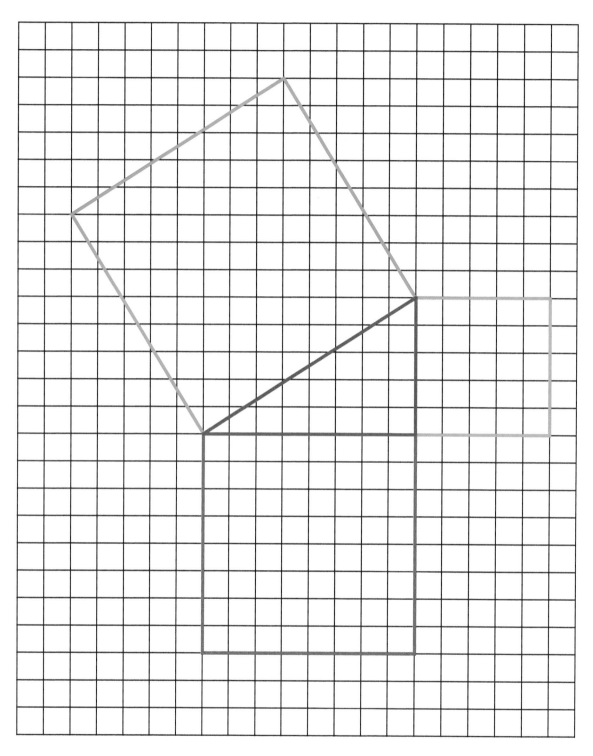

Pythagorean Triples

Snapshot

Students play with patterns in Pythagorean triples—right triangles with whole-number side lengths.

 Connection to CCSS
8.G.6, 8.G.7, 8.G.4

Agenda

Activity	Time	Description/Prompt	Materials
Launch	10–15 min	Show students the 3-4-5 Right Triangle sheet and ask them whether it is possible to have a right triangle with three whole-number side lengths. Students build the triangle to test this idea and share their representations. Come to agreement that this triangle is valid, and name right triangles with three whole-number side lengths as *Pythagorean triples*.	• 3-4-5 Right Triangle sheet, to display • Make available: tools for constructing, such as square tiles, snap cubes, or Cuisenaire rods
Play	30+ min	Partners use tools, such as square tiles and snap cubes, to search for more right triangles that can be made with three whole-number side lengths. Partners develop ways of testing the triples they find. Students record their findings and look for patterns.	• Grid or dot paper (see appendix) and ruler, per partnership • Tools for constructing, such as square tiles, snap cubes, or Cuisenaire rods, per partnership
Discuss	20 min	Develop a plan as a class for collecting all the triples students found into a class chart to look for patterns. Discuss the strategies students used for finding triples and the patterns they notice among them. Make connections to similarity.	Chart and markers

To the Teacher

In this activity, we step away from a focus on irrational numbers and square roots to explore a special set of right triangles with whole-number side lengths, also known as Pythagorean triples. These sets of three whole numbers are special because they satisfy the relationship $a^2 + b^2 = c^2$. Perhaps the most famous Pythagorean triple is the 3-4-5 right triangle, which we use to launch this activity. Notice the following:

$$3^2 + 4^2 = 5^2$$

$$9 + 16 = 25$$

Another frequently cited Pythagorean triple is the 5-12-13 right triangle.

$$5^2 + 12^2 = 13^2$$

$$25 + 144 = 169$$

Of course, any triangle similar to either of these will also be a Pythagorean triple. That is, if you applied a whole-number scale factor by multiplying all of the side lengths by 2, 3, and so on, the results would be a new, larger right triangle with three whole-number side lengths. We encourage you to test this out yourself. It is this pattern, which connects the ideas of the Pythagorean theorem and similarity, that we hope students will play with in this activity.

We encourage you to make available tools for students to build and test right triangles with whole-number side lengths. Students may want to draw on grid paper, but they are very likely to create a vast series of triangles with two whole-number legs and an irrational hypotenuse. If, instead, students start with whole-number units in the form of snap cubes, Cuisenaire rods, or square tiles, they can add or subtract them to see whether they can make a right triangle.

Activity

Launch

Launch the activity by showing students the 3-4-5 Right Triangle sheet on the document camera. Remind students that in their exploration of the Pythagorean theorem in the Visualize activity, they encountered a lot of right triangles where the hypotenuse had an irrational side length. Ask, Is it possible to have a right triangle with all whole-number side lengths like this? Invite students to try to build this triangle to confirm or refute whether it is possible. Make available the same materials you will offer for the Explore portion of this lesson for students to choose from.

Invite students to share their constructions as evidence, and come to agreement that this triangle does indeed work. Tell students that this is a famous right triangle, because the side lengths are whole numbers (positive integers), and no irrational numbers are needed. Right triangles such as this one are called *Pythagorean triples*.

Play

Provide partners with grid or dot paper (see appendix) and ruler, and tools for constructing, such as square tiles, snap cubes, or Cuisenaire rods. Students explore the following questions:

- What other right triangles can you find that have three whole-number side lengths?
- If you find a set of three whole-number side lengths that you think makes a right triangle, how could you test it to confirm that it works?
- What patterns can you find in these Pythagorean triples?
- Can you use these patterns to create more right triangles with whole-number side lengths?

Discuss

As a class, discuss the following questions:

- How can we construct a class data table of all the triangles you found? (Come up with a class plan and collect all the triangles that students have discovered.)
- How did you search for Pythagorean triples? What strategies were useful?
- When you found a set of three side lengths that you thought were a triple, how did you test them to confirm whether they worked as a right triangle?
- What patterns did you notice? What patterns do you now see in our class table? (Annotate the class chart to highlight connections or patterns.)
- How can you use these patterns to generate more Pythagorean triples?
- What are you wondering now?

In the discussion, be sure to highlight the pattern of similarity when it surfaces. You might ask, Will all triangles similar to a Pythagorean triple (such as the 3-4-5) be Pythagorean triples, too? Why or why not?

Look-Fors

- **How are students searching for triples?** Although it is possible for students to search for Pythagorean triples using grid paper and checking the length of the hypotenuse through calculation, this method is likely to be less efficient than more concrete methods. Encourage students to try building these right triangles with the tools you have available. Students can play with the side lengths, making them longer or shorter to try to make a whole-number hypotenuse fit. The challenge when using concrete tools is maintaining the right angle and knowing when the side lengths fit precisely (rather than fitting approximately). You might ask, How could you make sure that you have a right angle? What tools could you use? Students might overlay their tools on grid paper or place an index card in the right angle.

- **Are students using what they know about right triangles to check the triples they find?** Given that constructing right triangles with concrete tools inevitably introduces error, students will need to develop methods for checking that the triples they have identified actually make a right triangle. Students might choose to draw on the Pythagorean theorem as a tool for checking, finding the sum of the squares of the two legs and comparing that to the square of the hypotenuse. Alternatively, students could draw their triangle on grid paper, such that the legs are whole numbers, and then draw a square where the hypotenuse is one side. They can use this square, as they did in previous activities, to find the side length and compare it to their findings with manipulatives. Ask, How could you check to see whether this triple actually makes a right triangle? How could you use what you know about the side lengths of right triangles to help you?

- **Are students making connections to similarity?** One key pattern we are hoping students might discover is that Pythagorean triples can be scaled up to create new, similar Pythagorean triples. Students may discover this conceptually, by wondering what might happen if they double the side lengths of the 3-4-5 right triangle. Alternatively, students might create triples and then look for patterns. To do this, a system for organizing the data will help students detect relationships, such as a table with three columns for the shorter leg, the longer leg, and the hypotenuse. If students discover this relationship through the numbers, ask them why this might work.

Reflect

How many Pythagorean triples do you think exist? Why?

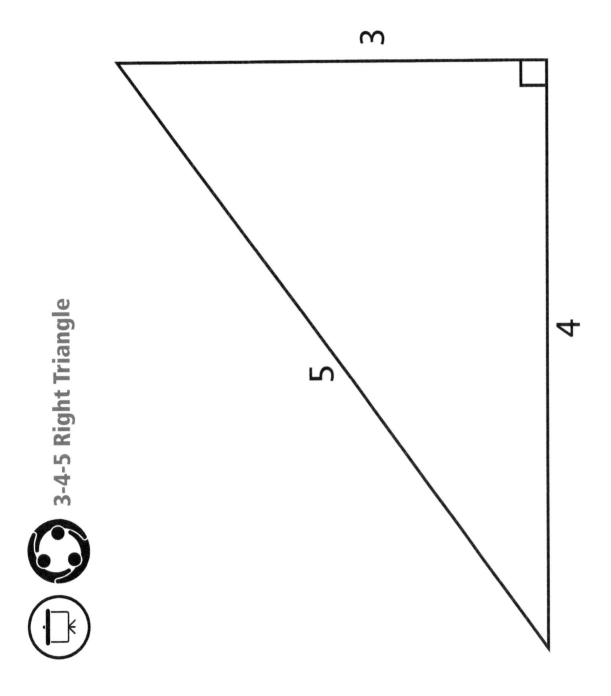

3-4-5 Right Triangle

3

4

5

Approximating Square Roots

Snapshot

Students use paper folding to explore the relationship between right triangles and square roots, and then to create a number line that includes the square roots of 1 through 16 to compare their lengths.

Connection to CCSS
8.NS.2, 8.G.8

Agenda

Activity	Time	Description/Prompt	Materials
Launch	10–15 min	Tell students that humans think of numbers as a distance or position, pointing out that 5 is halfway between 4 and 6. Ask, Is $\sqrt{5}$ halfway between $\sqrt{4}$ and $\sqrt{6}$? Show students a square piece of paper folded into a 4 x 4 grid. Ask where student see right triangles on this grid.	Patty or origami paper, folded into a 4 x 4 grid
Explore	40+ min	Partners make their own 4 x 4 grid and use it to find distances such as $\sqrt{2}$ and $\sqrt{3}$. They use this tool to construct a number line showing the relative positions of all square roots from $\sqrt{1}$ to $\sqrt{16}$. Students investigate the relationships in their number line and how they might extend it to find larger square roots, such as $\sqrt{40}$.	Patty or origami paper, ruler, compass, and colors, per partnership
Discuss	20+ min	Invite students to share the number lines they constructed. Discuss the strategies students used, the relationships between square roots on the number line, and how students might extend their number lines.	

To the Teacher

In this activity, we venture to approximate square roots by placing them on a number line. We approach this, as we have with other activities related to square roots, through geometry, so that students are able to see square roots as numbers that can be compared. Placing irrational numbers on a number line puts them in relation to one another, to whole numbers, and to all rational numbers.

The tool we use for this is a simple folded piece of square paper. You can use either origami paper or patty paper, folding it into a 4 × 4 grid, and for the launch you'll need to have one of these ready to share. The folded grid creates units and unit squares. These units do not correspond to standard units of measure; instead they define a scale for creating a number line. Each edge of the folded paper could be a number line, with the units 1, 2, 3, and 4 marked by the folds and the perpendicular edge.

A square piece of origami paper is folded in half four times to create a 4 × 4 square grid.

The grid creates units, but also unit squares, which are the building blocks for right triangles. As we have explored in previous activities, the hypotenuses of these right triangles have lengths that can be found using the side square or the Pythagorean theorem. On a 4 × 4 grid, the grid can be used to find every square root length from $\sqrt{1}$ (the side length of one unit square) to $\sqrt{32}$ (the length of the diagonal). In this activity, we start by asking students to create a number line of the square roots from $\sqrt{1}$ to $\sqrt{16}$, because these fit on the edge of the paper. Some students may find that they want to make their number line directly on their 4×4 folded square, though this is not required. We've asked that students have access to compasses to help them transfer the length of each hypotenuse to their number lines.

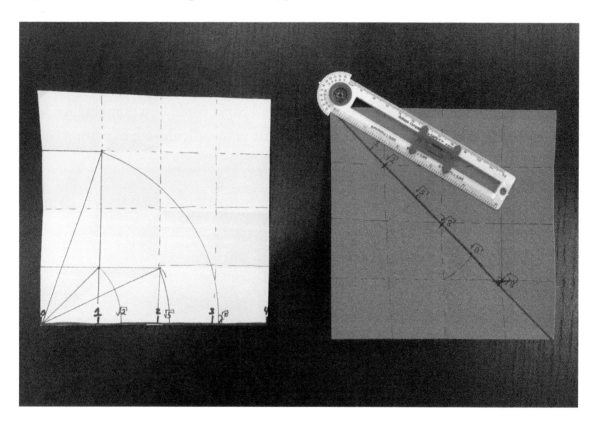

Student work showing the use of a compass to approximate the rectangle diagonal length on a number line. Without a compass, students can approximate the diagonal length by folding.

We encourage you to try this activity yourself to discover which square roots are more challenging to locate and the work it takes to create the number line.

Activity

Launch

Launch the activity by telling students that neuroscientists have found that people hold numbers on a number line in the visual part of their brain. This means that we understand numbers as a distance or as a location relative to other numbers. Tell students that, for example, they know that 4 is 1 unit away from 5 and that 5 is halfway between 4 and 6. You might draw a short number line to point out these whole-number relationships. Tell students that now, after the work they have done with irrational numbers, they know that $\sqrt{4}$ is less than $\sqrt{16}$. Ask, But where are these on the number line? How far apart are they? Is $\sqrt{5}$ halfway between $\sqrt{4}$ and $\sqrt{6}$?

Show students your 4×4 folded square of paper on the document camera. Be sure to point out that in this grid, each square is a unit, but these are not standard units like inches. Ask, Where are there right triangles on this paper? Give students a chance to turn and talk to a partner. Invite students to come up to show several places where they see right triangles embedded in the grid. Be sure that someone points out a right triangle that isn't isosceles, and if no one does, you might ask, Can anyone find a right triangle that isn't isosceles?

Explore

Provide partners with patty or origami paper, ruler, compass, and colors. Partners begin by folding their paper into a 4×4 grid. Students use this as their tool, with the squares in the grid as their units, to explore the following questions:

- If each of the 16 squares in your grid is 1 unit long, how long is $\sqrt{2}$? How long is $\sqrt{3}$?
- How can you use your 4×4 paper to construct a number line that shows all the square roots from $\sqrt{1}$ to $\sqrt{16}$?
- Are there any square root values you cannot find in your grid? Why or why not?
- What do you notice about the relationships among the locations of the square roots on your number line? Is $\sqrt{5}$ halfway between $\sqrt{4}$ and $\sqrt{6}$, for example?

Students may choose to construct their number line directly on the origami or patty paper or on a separate sheet of blank paper.

- What larger square roots could you add to your number line using your 4×4 folded paper? Add as many square roots as you can.
- What would you need in order to draw the length of a much larger square root, such as $\sqrt{40}$?
- How could you extend your number line?
- What does your number line make you wonder?

Invite students to share their number lines on the document camera. As a class, discuss the following questions:

- How did you construct your number lines?
- How did you find the location of each square root?
- Which square roots were easier or harder to locate? Why?
- Were there any you could not find? Why?
- Looking at the number line, what do you notice about the positions of the square roots? What relationships do you see? Where are the square roots located in relationship to the integers?
- How would you extend your number line beyond $\sqrt{16}$?
- If you did extend your number line, what patterns would you expect to see? Why?
- What do you wonder now about irrational numbers?

Look-Fors

- **Are students using the folded paper as a measurement tool? Do they see the units on the grid as numbers?** The premise of this task is that the folded square creates a new system of units, in which each of the squares on the 4×4 grid can be thought of as 1 unit long. It is in this system that the values of all the other measures make sense. If you notice students using rulers to measure the lengths of rectangles or triangles, press students to talk about what they are measuring and why. Remind them that in this problem, the grid makes a new numbering system, so inches and centimeters aren't relevant.

- **Do students see the hypotenuse of a right triangle as a length equivalent to a square root number?** Embedded in the grid are dozens of right triangles, each of which has a hypotenuse that could be useful for finding a square root length. Just as students need to see each square on the folded grid as a 1×1 square, they need to see the diagonals as the hypotenuses of right triangles that have a certain length. Each length has a value, and that value is often an irrational number. Students need to connect these three ideas together: hypotenuse, length or distance, and square root value. Ask students questions to support them in connecting these ideas so that they can ultimately map the lengths they find onto a number line. You might ask, for example, Where in your triangle is $\sqrt{5}$? What does it mean that the hypotenuse is $\sqrt{5}$? What does that tell you about the value of $\sqrt{5}$?

- **How are students transferring their measures to a number line?** In our experience doing this activity with young people, many struggle with how to take the lengths they find on the grid they have created and transfer them onto a number line. We have seen students use the edge of the paper itself as a number line, as it is already subdivided into whole-number units from 0 to 4. We have also seen students fold a diagonal on their paper and use that fold as the number line; and sometimes students want a completely separate space for their number line, and they plot it on a blank sheet of paper. In many cases, though, students struggle with how to take a length they have found, say $\sqrt{5}$, which is the hypotenuse of a right triangle with legs 1 and 2 units in length, and transfer it to the number line they have created. If students simply want to swing a length down to the edge or up to the diagonal on the square paper, a compass can support accuracy. But many students don't see that they can simply hold their paper against the number line to transfer this length. If you see students struggling with this, ask, How are you going to transfer that length onto the number line accurately? What tools or strategies could help? You can invite students to get ideas by walking around to look at how others are accomplishing this.

- **Are students understanding that the square roots of perfect squares are whole numbers?** Sometimes students become so focused on the irrational numbers, they overlook that some square roots have rational values. If students plot all of their values as square roots, including $\sqrt{1}$, $\sqrt{4}$, $\sqrt{9}$, and $\sqrt{16}$, ask, What is another way to write these numbers? or What do we know about these numbers? The goal is not to replace these values, but to establish their equivalence. Alternatively, some students may get stuck trying to find a triangle with a hypotenuse that is $\sqrt{9}$ units in length. Again, you might ask, What do we know about this number that could help us?

Reflect

How big do you think $\sqrt{60}$ is? How could you figure it out without calculating it?

Exploring the Geometry of Ice Cream

Our last big idea of the Grade 8 book takes us back to the beginning of the book, with spatial and geometric thinking. With this content area, as with all of mathematics, it is important for students to experience the ideas physically. There are different brain areas that are available to students, and when students experience mathematical ideas physically, with movement, they embody them in the visual-spatial parts of the brain. When we see students gesture to explain mathematical ideas, we know that the ideas are embedded in these parts of their brain. And when they experience ideas through both physical movement and numbers, as they will in this activity, important brain connections and brain communication result. There is an entire research field devoted to the learning of ideas through what is known as "embodied cognition," and Sian Beilock (2015) has a lovely book on the same topic, called *How the Body Knows Its Mind*. It presents fascinating research and ideas showing that movement is really important to mathematical—and other—knowledge. We also have a short paper on Youcubed that is devoted to this idea (Boaler, Chen, Williams, & Cordero, 2016).

In our Visualize activity, students will be asked to fill solids with water, sand, or rice. Students will then be asked to develop conjectures about the relationships. Instead of sharing formulas with students, we ask them to develop intuition about volume and to think deeply about volume relationships, thinking, for example, about the relationship between the volume of a cylinder and the volume of a cube of the same height. If students explore these relationships physically instead of abstractly, they will develop a deeper understanding of the relationships.

In our Play activity, students meet our Prism Collection sheet and think about what they know about finding the volume of solids. This time students work with nets, using these to work out volumes. They then get to create their own net of a cylinder with a bigger volume, thinking about the cool open question, What is the largest-volume cylinder whose net can be drawn on a single sheet of paper?

In our Investigate activity, students think about the volume of ice cream in different-size servings. We hope that students can draw on the chart of conjectures they developed in the Visualize activity as a resource for this investigation. Students are asked to develop methods for estimating the volume of ice cream in cups, then they are invited to design an ice cream cone and scoop with approximately the same volume as the cup. This is a complex investigation, and students will be helped by building and testing different models.

Jo Boaler

Reference

Beilock, S. (2015). *How the body knows its mind*. New York, NY: Simon & Schuster.

Boaler, J., Chen, L., Williams, C., & Cordero, M. (2016). Seeing as understanding: The importance of visual mathematics for our brain and learning. *Journal of Applied & Computational Mathematics, 5*, 5. doi:10.4172/2168-9679.1000325

Building Intuition about Volume

Snapshot

Students use fillable relational solids to explore and build conjectures about the relationships between their volumes.

Connection to CCSS
8.G.9

Agenda

Activity	Time	Description/Prompt	Materials
Launch	10 min	Show students a set of relational solids and ask students what they notice. Be sure the class has a shared vocabulary for the names of the solids and for ways of describing their dimensions. Be sure students notice that one dimension is the same for all of the solids.	Set of relational solids including a sphere, cone, cylinder, and cube, to display
Explore	25–30 min	Groups explore the relationships between the volumes of the solids by filling them with water, sand, or rice. Students develop conjectures about the relationships and evidence to support their ideas.	• Set of fillable relational solids, including a sphere, cone, cylinder, and cube, per group • Filling substance, such as water, sand, or rice, in a broad container, per group
Discuss	20 min	Discuss and collect students' conjectures about the relationships between the volumes of the solids they explored. Press students to provide evidence from their explorations for their conjectures.	Chart and markers

To the Teacher

In middle school, students are often asked to work with volumes only abstractly, through formulas. Indeed, the standard for volume in eighth grade only asks students to "know the formulas" rather than understand them. The formulas for the volumes of solids with curves can become challenging to understand and quite complex, but as with all other formulas, remembering them is not the same as learning. We take a departure from the formulas entirely in this activity and instead focus on building intuition around volume, particularly relative volume. That is, how does the volume of a cylinder relate to volume of a cube of the same height? How are each of these related to the volume of a cone with the same height or a sphere with an equivalent diameter? These relationships are most readily explored, discovered, and understood physically, rather than abstractly.

Fillable relational geometric solids offer students the opportunity to conduct just these kinds of explorations. These manipulatives are hollow and have a hole for filling them with a substance such as water, sand, or rice. They are *relational* because they all have at least one shared dimension, usually the height. This means that, in the case of the cube and the cylinder, the difference is the base; when comparing the cone and the cylinder, the difference is the way the cone tapers. This allows students to build conjectures about the effect of changing the base shape or tapering the end to form a cone. Students can pour the filling substance from one solid to another to see how the volumes compare. In this activity, the goal is for students to get a felt sense of the differences between volumes of different types of solids, particularly those with curves. Students develop conjectures in this lesson about those relationships, which you can record on a chart and use in the remaining activities in this big idea.

Activity

Launch

Launch the activity by showing students a set of relational solids including a sphere, cone, cylinder, and cube. Ask students, What do you notice about these solids? Give students a chance to turn and talk to a partner, and then take some observations about the solids. In this discussion, be sure the class has a shared vocabulary for the names of these figures and how to describe their dimensions with words such as *height* and *diameter*. Be sure that students notice that one of the dimensions, the height (or diameter), is the same for all.

Explore

Provide each group with a set of fillable relational solids, including a sphere, cone, cylinder, and cube, and a filling substance such as water, sand, or rice in a broad container. Ask students to explore the relationships between the volumes of these figures by filling them and considering the following questions:

- What relationships can you find between the volumes of these figures?
- What conjectures can you make?
- What evidence can you generate for these conjectures?

Discuss

As a class, discuss the following questions:

- What relationships did you find between the volumes of these figures?
- What conjectures did your group make?
- What evidence can you offer for your conjectures? (Invite students to share evidence from their fillable solids by demonstrating the relationships they found.)
- If the solids were a different size—much larger or smaller—would the relationships you found still be true? Why or why not?

Make a chart of students' conjectures, focused on the relationships between the volumes of the solids, rather than on the volumes themselves. For instance, students might conjecture that the volume of a sphere is about $\frac{2}{3}$ of the volume of a cylinder with the same height and diameter.

Look-Fors

- **Are students pouring from one solid to another to make comparisons?** The key opportunity these solids offer is the chance to pour the volume from one solid into another. Students can ask questions such as, Which volume is bigger? If we pour the volume of a smaller solid into a larger solid, about what portion of the solid will be filled? If we pour the volume of a larger solid into a smaller solid, about how much volume is left over? Which solid might it make sense to compare the others to? We offer the cube so that students can use this as the definition of a cubic unit, as a reference for the others if they want. If you do not see students pouring volume from one solid to another, ask, How will you compare the volumes of these solids? How could you look for relationships between their volumes?

- **Are students posing questions they can test?** Encourage a space of wondering about volume during this activity. You want students to be asking questions of themselves and each other, such as, Which one do you think is the biggest or smallest? Do you think the cylinder and the sphere have the same volume? What about the cube and the sphere? How many times do you think we could pour the volume of the cone into the cube before it filled up? Each of these questions is intriguing and testable. Rather than posing these questions in a long list for students to tick off one by one, we hope that students will become curious and begin posing their own questions that will drive their exploration.

- **Are students using their findings to make conjectures or collect evidence?** With a physical activity like this one, it can be easy for students to focus solely on pouring volumes back and forth to explore questions. This is, as we've said, at the heart of what we want students to do. Along the way, however, encourage students to record their observations, evidence, and emerging conjectures so that their explorations can be captured for the class to consider. Ask, How could you record that observation? What do you think that might mean about the relationships between the volumes of these solids?

Reflect

What are you wondering now about the volume of curved solids, such as cylinders, cones, and spheres?

Comparing Cylinders

Snapshot

Students use the nets of cylinders and what they know about prisms to develop methods for finding the volume of cylinders.

Connection to CCSS
8.G.9

Agenda

Activity	Time	Description/Prompt	Materials
Launch	10 min	Show students the Prism Collection sheet and ask them what they know about finding the volume of solids like these. Show students the Cylinder Net sheet and ask, How could you use the information on this net to find the volume of the cylinder it creates?	• Prism Collection sheet, to display • Cylinder Net sheet, to display
Play	40+ min	Partners develop methods for finding the volume of a cylinder, using what they know about the volumes of prisms. Then students try to create a net for a cylinder that has an even larger volume. Students investigate the question, What is the largest-volume cylinder whose net can be drawn on a single sheet of paper?	• Cylinder Net sheet, copied on cardstock if possible, per partnership • Scissors, tape, compass, ruler, and blank card-stock, per partnership
Discuss	20+ min	Discuss the methods students developed for finding the volume of cylinders. Support students in generalizing a relationship that includes the area of the base and the height. Discuss students' strategies and evidence for constructing cylinder nets with an even larger volume.	

To the Teacher

In this activity, we create an opportunity for students to use what they know about other prisms to develop ways of finding the volume of a cylinder. We step away from filling solids physically and invite students to think about the similarity between cylinders and other right prisms. Unlike methods for measuring spheres and cones, the way we find the volume of cylinders is analogous to that for finding the volume of solids without curves. Just as with prisms, finding the volume of cylinders involves finding the area of the base and then multiplying that area by the height, as though cubes were being added layer upon layer from the base to the top. In fifth grade, we began working with cubic units to fill solids, but when figures involve curves, actually packing solids with cubes to find the volume introduces too much error. So in this lesson we ask students to connect what they know about prisms to develop abstract methods for finding the volume of cylinders.

You'll notice that we have not designated any units for students to use. Let students choose whether they want to use cubic centimeters or cubic inches. Across your classroom you may have groups making different choices, and this will come up in the discussion. Regardless of the units, the focus needs to be on the method.

Activity

Launch

Launch the activity by showing students the Prism Collection sheet on the document camera and asking, What do you know about finding the volume of solids like these, or prisms? Give students a chance to turn and talk to a partner, and then take students' ideas. This is intended to be a brief discussion that activates students' prior knowledge about the volume of prisms.

Show students the Cylinder Net sheet, and tell them that this is the net for a cylinder. It is made of two circles and a rectangle. Ask, how could you use just the information on this net to find the volume of the cylinder? Give students a chance to turn and talk to a partner.

Play

Provide partners the Cylinder Net sheet, copied on cardstock if possible, and scissors, tape, compass, ruler, and blank cardstock. Using these tools, students explore the following questions:

- Using what you know about the volume of other prisms, how can you find the volume of a cylinder?

- Can you create a cylinder net that is even larger, on a single sheet of paper?
- What is the largest-volume cylinder whose net can be drawn on a single sheet of paper?

Discuss

As a class, discuss the following questions:

- How can you find the volume of a cylinder?
- How does finding the volume of a cylinder relate to how we find the volumes of other prisms?
- How does the volume of a cylinder relate to the area of a circle?
- What is the volume of this cylinder? (Groups will likely have used different units of measure. If this happens, ask, How can we compare your results given the different units you used?)
- How did you think about making a cylinder net that had a larger volume? What was your strategy?
- How can you prove that your net has a larger volume than the cylinder on the net sheet?

Use this discussion to arrive at an agreement on a generalizable relationship between the dimensions of the cylinder and its volume. We usually express this relationship as a formula, but it is more important for students to understand the relationship than represent it with the symbols.

Look-Fors

- **Are students making conceptual connections between prisms and cylinders?** As discussed in the To the Teacher section, the central aim of this activity is for students to see cylinders as a special kind of prism, whose volume can be thought of in the same way as that of a rectangular solid. Look for evidence that students are thinking about the area of the base and layers of cubic units building up from the base to the top of the cylinder. You may even notice the ways students use hand gestures to talk about layering. If students seem stumped about how to think about the volume, ask questions that prompt students to connect these figures to prisms. You might ask, What do you know about finding the volume of other kinds of solids, such as rectangular solids? You might bring out the Prism Collection sheet or some of the relational solids as a tool for talking about the volume of these kinds of figures. Ask, How might that way of thinking about volume help with finding the volume of a cylinder? How are these figures alike?

- **Are students struggling to find the area of the circular base?** In seventh grade, we focused on building understanding of circles, including developing ways for finding area and understanding pi. However, if students have not worked with circles since then, they might struggle with thinking about the area of circles. Students may benefit from drawing a few circles on grid paper (see appendix) using their compass, and trying to find the circles' areas using the grid to remind themselves of the pattern: that circle area is the radius squared times pi. In seventh grade, we focused on the idea of the "radius square," or the square that can be created with the radius as the side length, and that a little more than three (that is, pi) of these squares cover the circle. Give students a chance to explore this idea again to reconstruct their understanding through looking at circles on a grid and talking to one another. If the entire class seems to be struggling, consider pausing the work with cylinders to talk about why the area of the base is needed. Consider this a crucial conceptual victory. Then ask the entire class to explore how you might find the area of a circle on a grid. You could even return to the seventh-grade Big Idea 10 Play activity in its entirety before diving back into cylinders.

Reflect

How can you find the volume of a cylinder? What information would you need? Why?

Prism Collection

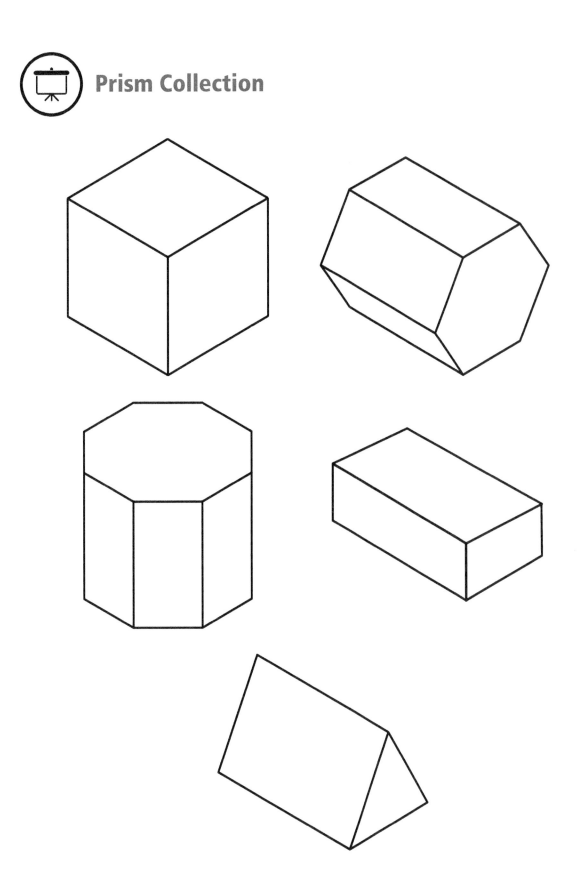

Cylinder Net

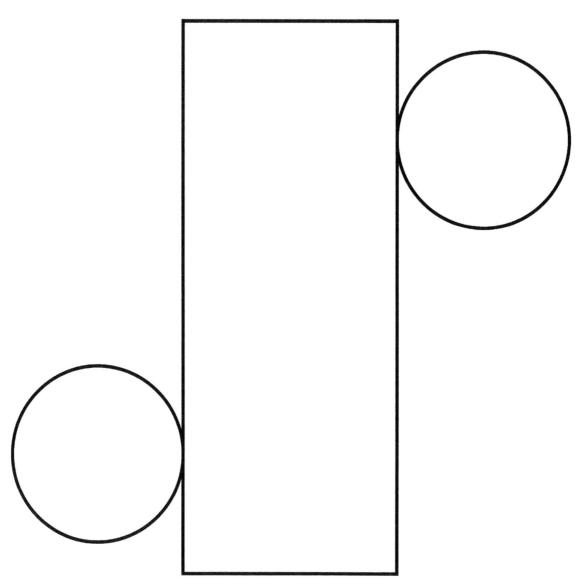

Scooping Up Volume

Snapshot

Students investigate ways of finding the volume of spheres and cones, building on their earlier conjectures, as they design ice cream cones with the same volume as cylindrical cups.

Connection to CCSS
8.G.9

Agenda

Activity	Time	Description/Prompt	Materials
Launch	10 min	Show students the Cup of Ice Cream sheet and ask, How could you figure out how much ice cream is in this serving? Discuss what students notice and what they think they might need to figure out. Point out the chart of conjectures about volume that the class created in the Visualize activity as a resource for this investigation.	• Cup of Ice Cream sheet, to display • Chart of conjectures about volume from the Visualize activity
Explore	60+ min	Partners develop methods for estimating the volume of ice cream in the cup shown. Then students design an ice cream cone and scoop with approximately the same volume as the cup. Students build and test models for their cone.	• Cup of Ice Cream sheet, per partnership • Make available: relational solid set, a filling material in a broad container, paper, scissors, and tape

Activity	Time	Description/Prompt	Materials
Discuss	20+ min	Discuss the methods that students developed for finding the volume of the cup of ice cream and compare estimates for that volume. Discuss the ways that students approached designing a cone with the same volume. Invite students to share and compare their designs, and their evidence that these cones have approximately the same volume as the cup.	
Extend	30–60 min	Invite groups to create their own ice cream shop in which the pricing for each cone or cup of ice cream is proportional to the volume of ice cream purchased. Students design the scoops, cones, and cups offered and the price for each.	Make available: relational solid set, a filling material in a broad container, paper, scissors, and tape

To the Teacher

In reading this activity, you'll notice that we are not focusing on the formulas for the volume of spheres and cones. Although students can use what they know about prisms to reason about methods for finding the volume of cylinders, as we did in the Play activity, the formulas for finding the volumes of cones and spheres are not natural extensions of the formulas for the volumes of other kinds of solids. Rather than focusing on the formulas themselves, with which student are always provided in testing contexts and which students do not need to memorize, we believe it is a better use of students' time to extend their thinking about the relative volumes of these figures in more complex problem-solving situations. The precision of students' answers is less important than the precision of their reasoning.

Students are invited first to build on their understanding of how to find the volume of a cylinder and on their conjectures that they developed in the Visualize activity to find the volume of a cup with a half-scoop of ice cream on top. Expect estimates for the half-sphere that extend from filling relational solids. Then we challenge students to design a cone with the same volume, whose height and diameter students can select. Removing the constraint that the cone must have the same diameter as the cup opens up the task to multiple possible solutions, but creates a much more challenging design task. We encourage you to make time for ample design and testing of cones, an activity that could easily extend across multiple days.

Activity

Launch

Launch the activity by showing students the Cup of Ice Cream sheet on the document camera. Tell students that the person who scooped the ice cream at this shop packed the ice cream into the container completely, with a scoop coming out the top. Ask, How much ice cream do you think is in this serving? How would you figure it out? Give students a chance to turn and talk to a partner. Take some students' observations about the figure and what might be needed to determine the volume of ice cream in this serving.

Point out the conjectures students made in the Visualize activity, which you recorded on a chart. Make sure this chart is visible as a reference for students. Tell students that these ideas might be useful to them today as they investigate the volume of ice cream.

Explore

Provide partners with the Cup of Ice Cream sheet and access to the relational solid set, a filling material (such as sand or rice) in a broad container, paper, scissors, and tape. Students may want to construct or fill solids to test their ideas. Students use these tools to investigate the following questions:

- What is the approximate volume of ice cream in the cup shown in the image?
- What methods can you develop for finding its volume?
- How precise do you think your estimates are? Why?

Then partners design a cone and scoop that will hold approximately the same volume of ice cream as the cup shown in the image. The cone must include a half-sphere scoop of ice cream on top. As they design their cone, students explore the following questions:

- What is the height of your cone? What is its diameter?
- How big is your scoop? How many scoops will you need?
- How can you be sure that the volume is the same as the cup of ice cream in the image? How close do you think your estimates are for the volume? Why?
- What other cones could you design with the same volume?

Encourage students to build their cones out of paper and test their ideas about the cone's volume by filling it.

Discuss

As a class, discuss the following questions:

- How did you find the volume of the cup of ice cream in the image?
- What was the approximate volume of the cup? How do our estimates compare?
- How did you design your cone(s)? What were your strategies?

Invite students to share the different cones they designed and discuss the following questions:

- What do our cones have in common? How are they different?
- How can we prove that they all have approximately the same volume?
- What surprises you about the cones you designed?

Extend

Ask students to imagine that they are designing an ice cream shop and that the pricing of cones and cups is proportional to the volume of ice cream a person buys. Make available a relational solid set, a filling material in a broad container, paper, scissors, and tape, for students who want to construct and test their ideas. Groups explore the following questions:

- What sizes of scoops, cones, and cups will you offer?
- How will you price them? Why?

Look-Fors

- **Are students using their conjectures to develop methods for estimating volume?** The chart the class made during the Visualize activity contains critical conjectures that can help students develop estimates for the volume of the half-spheres and cones in this task. Students should not expect that they need to find an exact volume, but these conjectures should provide enough reasoning for justification. For instance, students likely found that the volume of a cone is approximately $\frac{1}{3}$ that of a cylinder with the same height and radius. This turns out to be the precise relationship, rather than just an approximation. Similarly, students may have found that spheres have approximately $\frac{1}{3}$ more volume than a cylinder with the same radius and a height equal to the diameter. Again, it turns out that this is the precise relationship, with spheres having $\frac{4}{3}$ the volume of cylinders with the same dimensions. If students think proportionally, using these conjectures, they will be very accurate in their estimates.

However, if students' conjectures from the earlier activity were less precise, their estimates will be similarly less precise. You might use this investigation as an opportunity to test and revise the conjectures, by asking, Do you think we could test these conjectures to see whether the evidence supports them, before we use them to find the volumes in this investigation?

- **Are students reasoning precisely about the relationships between the volumes of solids?** It is important to the precision of students' reasoning that they keep in mind the conditions of the relationships between the volumes of these solids. For instance, a cone is $\frac{1}{3}$ the volume of a cylinder, *when* the cone and cylinder have the same radius and height. If those conditions change, the relationship is no longer true. In the Visualize activity, these conditions were fixed in the relational solids, so students didn't need to grapple with them explicitly. But when designing their cones, they have the authority to choose the radius and the height of the cone, and in doing so, they are intentionally changing the relationship between the volume of that cone and the volume of the cylinder.

- **Are students making assumptions about the constraints for designing their cones?** Given our previous work with solids that have the same height and radius, students may assume that these are constraints when designing their cones. Although it may be conceptually helpful to keep the radius the same for the cone and the cylinder (because this will also make the half-spheres equal), if students assume that the cone needs to have the same height, the problem becomes unsolvable. Remind students that they can choose the radius and height of the cone, and ask, What height (or radius) might make your cone and scoop have the same volume as the cup and scoop? What is the relationship if they have the same height and radius? How might you use that relationship to choose a design to test?

Reflect

What relationships between the volumes of cylinders, cones, and spheres do you think will be the most useful to you in the world? Why?

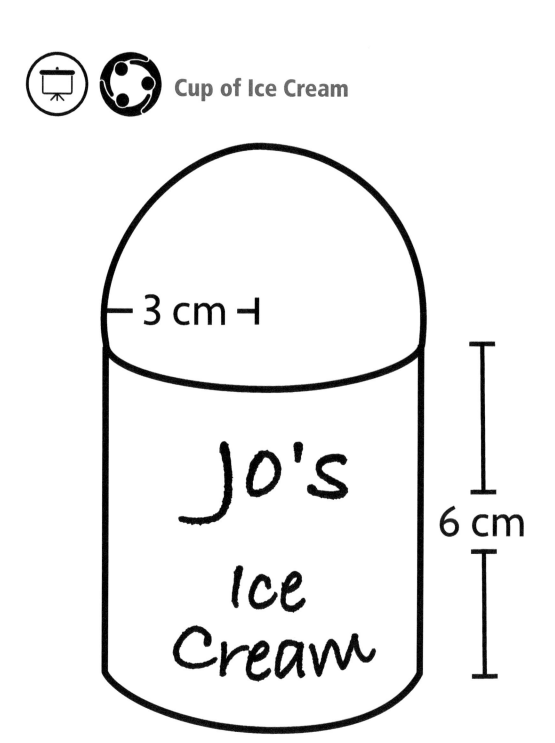
— 3 cm —|

Jo's
Ice
Cream

6 cm

Appendix

Centimeter Grid Paper

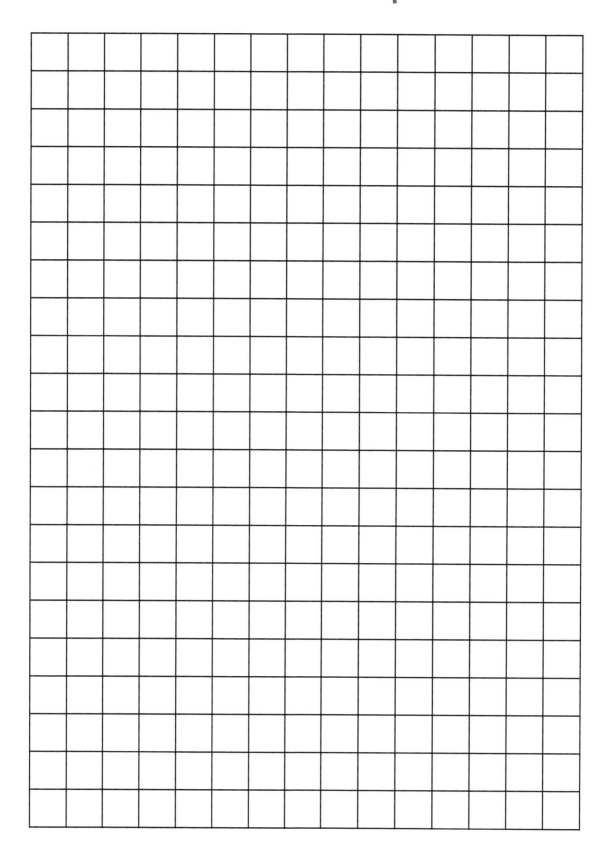

Appendix

Grid Paper

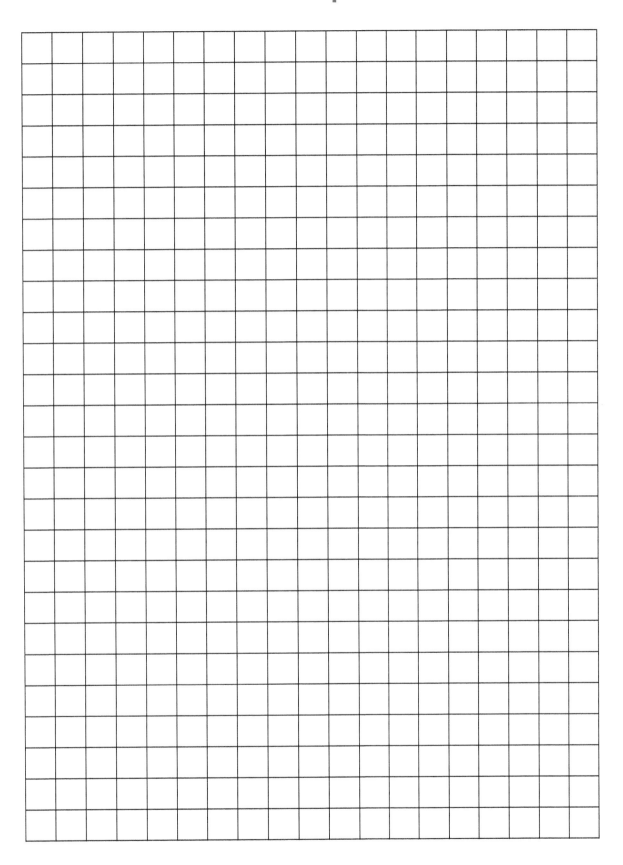

Isometric Dot Paper

Appendix

Dot Paper

.

About the Authors

Dr. Jo Boaler is a professor of mathematics education at Stanford University, and the cofounder of Youcubed. She is the author of the first MOOC on mathematics teaching and learning. Former roles have included being the Marie Curie Professor of Mathematics Education in England, a mathematics teacher in London comprehensive schools, and a lecturer and researcher at King's College, London. Her work has been published in the *Times,* the *Telegraph,* the *Wall Street Journal,* and many other news outlets. The BBC recently named Jo one of the eight educators "changing the face of education."

Jen Munson is an assistant professor of learning sciences at Northwestern University, a professional developer, and a former classroom teacher. She received her PhD from Stanford University. Her research focuses on how coaching can support teachers in growing their mathematics instructional practices and how teacher-student interactions influence equitable math learning. She is the author of *In the Moment: Conferring in the Elementary Math Classroom*, published by Heinemann.

Cathy Williams is the cofounder and director of Youcubed. She completed an applied mathematics major at University of California, San Diego before becoming a high school math teacher for 18 years in San Diego County. After teaching, she became a county office coordinator and then district mathematics director. As part of her leadership work, Cathy has designed professional development and curriculum. Her district work in the Vista Unified School District won a California Golden Bell for instruction in 2013 for the K–12 Innovation Cohort in mathematics. In Vista, Cathy worked with Jo changing the way mathematics was taught across the district.

Acknowledgments

We thank Jill Marsal, our book agent, and the team at Wiley for their efforts to make these books what we'd imagined. We are also very grateful to our Youcubed army of teachers. Thanks to Robin Anderson for drawing the network diagram on our cover. Finally, we thank our children—and dogs!—for putting up with our absences from family life as we worked to bring our vision of mathematical mindset tasks to life.

Index

Altitude, 73, 75

Analysis, 71–72

Angle rulers, 18

Angles, 89

Animation, 47, 49

Approximating square roots, 214–219

Area, 178, 179, 181–182, 230

Arguments, 30–31

Assumptions, 237

B

Balls, 18

Before and after sheet, 37, 41

Beilock, Sian, 221

Between 4 × 4 and 5 × 5, 187–192

Big ideas, 9; discovering Pythagoras as, 201–203; exploring the geometry of ice cream as, 221–222; functions as, 117–119; growth patterns as, 91–92; moving shapes as, 27–28; real number system as, 177–178, 188; zooming in and out as, 53–54

Bivariate data, 152–153

Boaler, Jo. *See* Big ideas

Brain science. *See* Neuroscience

Brainstorming, 21

Building intuition about volume, 223–226

Building norms, 21–25

C

Calculators, 19

Card stock, 19

Case numbers, 95–96, 117–118, 137–138. *See also* Functions; Growing functions

Centimeter grid paper, 240

Chain pattern sheet, 45–46, 51

Challenge: with area, 230; discussion of, 39; with geometry, 23; in identification, 63; for partners, 124; in play, 178; questions for, 87, 109, 210–211; from relationships, 138; for students, 14, 50, 63, 83, 95, 104–105, 212; transformations as, 36

Change, 98, 101, 104, 105

Chart paper, 35, 107

Charts, 67

Climate graph, 151, 153

Color-coding, 6–7, 102, 109–110, 134, 144–145

Colors, 19

Comparisons, 57, 62, 98, 225–232

Compasses, 18

Compression, 5

Conceptual connections, 229–230

Conceptual engagement, 4–5

Cones, 234–235. *See also* Cylinders

Congruence, 29–32, 82

Conjectures, 223, 225–226, 235, 236–237

Connections: conceptual, 229–230; after play, 112; with right triangles, 89; from similarity, 209, 212; strategies for, 82; from thinking, 196

Convincing, 5–8, 30–31

Coordinate planes, 31, 34, 68, 79, 89, 126

Cordero, Montse, 1

Counting, 95–98

Creating data visualizations, 166–175

Creativity: activities with, 74; with data, 110; discussion and, 223; with DIY transformations sheet, 36; for engagement, 11–12; in extension, 121; for group work, 87, 158, 234; in investigation, 28, 72; learning and, 5–6, 230; for partners, 81–82; with patterns, 104; in play, 150; relationships and, 235–236; with slope, 88–89; stories as, 150, 158–161; of students, 76, 109, 134; with triple triangle directions sheet, 73; in visualization, 144

Critical questions, 155–156

190–191; in the functions of near squares, 145–146; in getting warmer!, 137–138; in growing functions, 125–126; in growing on a grid, 68–69; in the hypotenuse hypothesis, 196–197; in pixel puzzles, 39–40; in Pythagorean triples, 212; in scooping up volume, 236–237; in seeing triangles under the line, 82–83; from skip-counting arrays, 104–105; in slide it, flip it, turn it, 49–50; in square sides, 182–183; from squared squares, 97–98; in stacking pennies, 111–112; in stairway to eleven, 88–89; in unpacking Pythagoras, 206–207; for what does it mean to be the same, 32; for what is similarity?, 57–58; in what's going on in this graph?, 155–156; from what's the story here?, 161–162

Low-floor tasks, 2–3

M

Magnitude, 39

Make the change sheet, 38, 43

Make your own function sheets, 121, 132–133

Manipulatives, 17–19. *See also specific manipulatives*

Masking tape, 19

Materials, 17–19

Math: The Having of Wonderful Ideas (Duckworth) about, 201–202; investigation of, 91; learning and, 3–4; *Math with Bad Drawings* (Orlin), 177; mathematical phenomena, 202; in neuroscience, 9–10; opening mathematics, 13–14; thinking about, 5–8; WIM for, 4, 11–12

Measurements, 57, 219

Memorization, 2, 4–5, 11, 118–119

Menon, Vinod, 9

Metacognition, 54

Meter sticks, 18

Methods, 9, 195, 227–228, 233–234

Middle School, 17

Movement, 101

Moving shapes, 27–28

Multiplication tables, 118–119, 141–148

Mystery scatterplot sheet, 158–161, 163

N

Name the change sheet, 37, 42

Near squares, 143–145

Negative cases, 118, 138

Neuroscience: learning in, 2, 221–222; math in, 9–10; of memorization, 11; of relationships, 53

New York Times, 151–156, 167–168

Numbers: case, 95–96, 117–118, 137–138; color-coding for, 109; on grid paper, 190; irrational, 177–178, 187–188, 190, 215–216; number lines, 10, 187, 189–190, 214–219; number visuals sheet, 111, 115; observations with, 103; patterns for, 71–72, 124; pi, 177; real number system, 177–178; relationships between, 125–126; sequences of, 71–72; thinking about, 214

O

Observations, 12, 38, 65, 86, 103, 224

OECD. *See* Organisation for Economic Co-operation and Development

Office supplies, 19

Online education, 1, 9

Online resources, 152

Squared right triangles sheet, 204–205, 208

Squares: area of, 181–182; functions of, 140–146; perfect squares, 219; square sides, 179–186; square tiles, 18; squared squares, 93–99

Stacking pennies, 107–113

Stairway to eleven, 85–90

Statistics, 159–160

Stories, 150, 158–161

Strategies: for connections, 82; for counting, 97–98; discussion of, 36, 61, 179, 182; efficacy of, 62; for pattern recognition, 146; students and, 39, 214, 236; visualization of, 190

Strogatz, Steve, 71, 117–118

Students: activities for, 9; algebra for, 117; assumptions by, 237; big ideas for, 9; case numbers for, 137–138; chain pattern sheet for, 46; challenge for, 14, 50, 63, 83, 95, 104–105, 212; color-coding for, 6–7; comparisons by, 98, 225–226; congruence for, 29, 82; conjectures by, 223, 225, 235; creativity of, 76, 109, 134; debates by, 38; descriptions by, 38; designs by, 89; engagement of, 3, 10–11; explanations by, 207; exploration by, 65–66, 79, 85, 88, 151; extension for, 86; gallery walks for, 48, 97–98; generalizations by, 142–143; identification by, 57; inferring by, 155; investigation by, 14–15, 47, 65, 72, 107, 118–119, 166, 178, 203, 222; irrational numbers for, 187; journaling for, 5–6; memorization for, 2; metacognition for, 54; in middle School, 17; multiplication tables for, 140–141; organization by, 111–112; paper folding for, 214; patterns for, 45, 68; PISA, 4; play for, 13–14, 60, 68, 158; point-by-point triangle sheet for, 30–31; proportions for, 58; questions for, 25, 36–37, 181; reasoning for, 22–23, 125; rules by, 49; similar triangles sheet for, 55–56; skepticism of, 8; stories by, 150, 158–161; strategies and, 39, 214, 236; teachers and, 12, 21, 91; 3 × 3 square sheet for, 93; transformations for, 35, 39–40; in US, 27; visualization for, 9–13, 61, 120, 179

Su, Francis, 119

Summer camp, 3–4

Surprises, 50

Symbols, 121–122

T

Tape, 19

Tasks, 2–3, 12–13, 120, 122–123, 127, 190

Teachers: approximating square roots for, 215–216; building intuition about volume for, 224; comparing cylinders for, 228; creating data visualizations for, 167–169; dropping the altitude for, 74; find the fakes for, 61; between 4 × 4 and 5 × 5 for, 188; the functions of near squares for, 141–143; getting warmer! for, 135–136; growing functions for, 121–122; growing on a grid for, 65–66; the hypotenuse hypothesis for, 194–195; materials for, 17–19; pixel puzzles for, 36–37; Pythagorean triples for, 210; questions by, 39; research for, 1; rules for, 27; scooping up

190; for students, 9–13, 61, 120, 179

Volume, 223–226, 229–230, 233–238. *See also* Cylinders

W

Week of inspirational mathematics (WIM), 4, 11–12

What does it mean to be the same, 29–34

What is similarity?, 55–59

What's going on in this graph?, 151–157, 167–168

What's the story here?, 158–165

Williams, Cathy, 1–2, 92

WIM. *See* Week of inspirational mathematics

Women in congress sheet, 158, 164

Work stations, 62

Y

Yardsticks, 18

Youcubed, 1, 3–4, 11–12

Z

Zero cases, 118

Zooming in and out, 53–54